Financial Terms Dictionary

Corporate Finance Explained

Published June 30, 2017

Revision 1.1

Financial Terms Dictionary

Copyright And Trademark Notices

Limits of Liability and Disclaimer of Warranties

The materials in this book are provided "as is" and without warranties of any kind either express or implied. The Author disclaims all warranties, express or implied, including, but not limited to, implied warranties of merchantability and fitness for a particular purpose.

The Author does not warrant that defects will be corrected, or that that the site or the server that makes this eBook available are free of viruses or other harmful components. The Author does not warrant or make any representations regarding the use or the results of the use of the materials in this book in terms of their correctness, accuracy, reliability, or otherwise. Applicable law may not allow the exclusion of implied warranties, so the above exclusion may not apply to you.

Under no circumstances, including, but not limited to, negligence, shall the Author be liable for any special or consequential damages that result from the use of, or the inability to use this eBook, even if the Author or his authorised representative has been advised of the possibility of such damages.

Applicable law may not allow the limitation or exclusion of liability or incidental or consequential damages, so the above limitation or exclusion may not apply to you. In no event shall the Author's total liability to you for all damages, losses, and causes of action (whether in contract, tort, including but not limited to, negligence or otherwise) exceed the amount paid by you, if any, for this eBook.

Facts and information are believed to be accurate at the time they were placed in this book. All data provided in this book is to be used for information purposes only. The information contained within is not intended to provide specific legal, financial or tax advice, or any other advice whatsoever, for any individual or company and should not be relied upon in that regard. The services described are only offered in jurisdictions where they may be legally offered. Information provided is not all-inclusive, and is limited to information that is made available and such information should not be relied upon as all-inclusive or accurate.

You are advised to do your own due diligence when it comes to making business decisions and should use caution and seek the advice of qualified professionals. You should check with your accountant, lawyer, or professional advisor, before acting on this or any information. You may not consider any examples, documents, or other content in this eBook or otherwise provided by the Author to be the equivalent of professional advice.

The Author assumes no responsibility for any losses or damages resulting from your use of any link, information, or opportunity contained in this book or within any other information disclosed by the author in any form whatsoever.

About the Author

Thomas Herold is a successful entrepreneur and personal development coach. After a career with one of the largest electronic companies in the world, he realised that a regular job would never fully satisfy his need for connection on a deep level. The only way to live his full potential was to start building his own business and find new ways to be in service to others.

For over 25 years he has helped many people - including himself - build their dream businesses. Toward that goal, he focuses on education, simplified and enhanced by modern technology. He is the author of 15 books with over 200,000 copies distributed worldwide.

Other than his passion for creating businesses, Thomas has spent over 20 years in the self-development field. Placing emphasis on the exploration of consciousness and building practical applications that allow people to express their purpose and passion in life, Thomas's work in this area has provided ample and happy proof that this approach works.

He believes that every person has at least one gift and that, when this gift is developed and nourished, it will serve as a fountainhead of personal happiness and help contribute to a better, more sustainable world.

For the past twelve years Thomas has studied the monetary system and has experienced some profound insights on how money and wealth are related. He has recently committed to sharing this financial knowledge in a new venture - the Financial Terms Dictionary, a hub of financial term descriptions designed to help people get started on their own money makeover and get a financial education in the process.

Thomas's ultimate vision for the Financial Terms Dictionary is to empower people to adopt a wealthy mindset and to create abundance for themselves and others. His ability to explain complex information in simple terms makes him an outstanding teacher and coach.

For more information please visit: Financial Terms Dictionary

Financial Dictionary Series

There are 12 books in this financial dictionaries series available. Click the links below to see an overview and available formats. There is also a premium edition available, which covers over 900 financial terms!

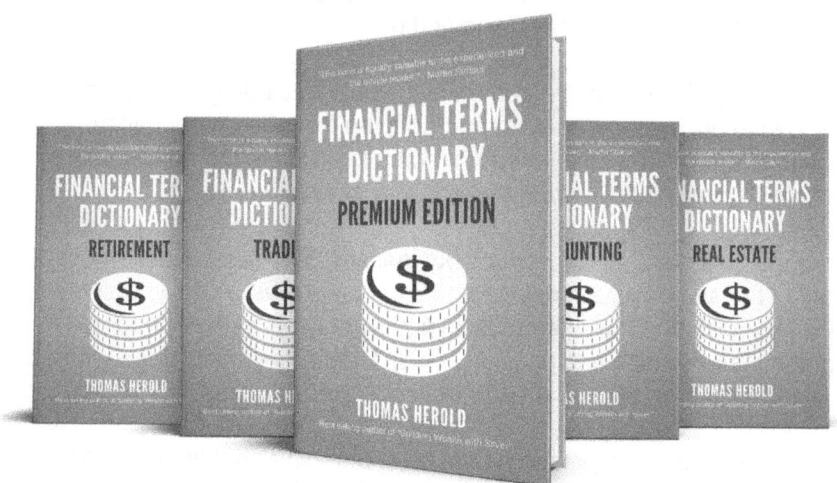

Standard Editions
Financial Terms Dictionary - Accounting Edition
Financial Terms Dictionary - Banking Edition
Financial Terms Dictionary - Corporate Finance Edition
Financial Terms Dictionary - Economics Edition
Financial Terms Dictionary - Investment Edition
Financial Terms Dictionary - Laws & Regulations Edition
Financial Terms Dictionary - Real Estate Edition
Financial Terms Dictionary - Retirement Edition
Financial Terms Dictionary - Trading Edition
Financial Terms Dictionary - Acronyms Edition

Basic & Premium Editions
Financial Terms Dictionary - Basic Edition
Financial Terms Dictionary - Premium Edition

Table Of Contents

AAA Rating

AAA Rating refers to the maximum potential credit rating that a credit ratings bureau can award to an issuing entity's bonds. Such a credit rating represents a superb level of creditworthiness. It means that the issuing entity is easily capable of meeting its various financial obligations. The three major ratings agencies of Moody's, Standard & Poor's, and Fitch Ratings all utilize the AAA as their top credit rating which designates those bonds and issuers which have the highest possible level of credit quality.

It is not possible to completely eliminate the potential risk of a credit default from a bond issuer. Yet those entities which possess AAA rated bonds are believed to have the least possible chance of defaulting on their interest payments or principal repayments. Because of this, such bonds provide their investors with the smallest possible yields of any bonds that possess the same dates of maturity.

Thanks to the Global Financial Crisis of 2008, many companies and countries lost their coveted AAA rating. In fact, by the middle of 2009, there were only four remaining firms out of the entire list of S&P 500 companies that still held their treasured AAA rated credit. The story was the same with the gold standard credit rated nations of the world as well.

Before the Great Recession, a number of nations enjoyed the highly coveted AAA credit rating from all three of the big three ratings agencies. Once the dust had settled, only the following nine nations still held it including Australia, Canada, Denmark, Germany, Luxembourg, Norway, Singapore, Sweden, and Switzerland. Countries that had lost it included Austria, Finland, France, the United Kingdom, and the United States. The U.S. still had the AAA rated credit from Moody's and Fitch, while the United Kingdom still held it from Standard & Poor's (who even removed it from negative watch).

High credit ratings like the AAA rating provide significant benefits to a company or nation which carries them. It allows the issuer to borrow at a reduced interest rate and ultimate cost. These companies and countries are also able to borrow greater amounts of money when they possess the highest ratings. Lower costs of borrowing allow for nations and corporations to access opportunities through cheap and easy credit. A company might be able to buy out a competitor as it is able to cheaply borrow the money for the transaction costs of the relevant merger and acquisition.

Where companies are concerned, it is possible for them to enjoy the highest AAA rating on bonds which they issue as secured while having a lower credit rating on those which are unsecured. This is simply because secured bonds provide a particular asset that has been put up as collateral in case the issuer defaults on the interest or principal payments of the bond in question. The creditor has the right to seize the asset if the issuer ends up defaulting. Such bonds could carry the collateral of real estate, machinery, or other forms of equipment. Conversely, unsecured bonds only carry the backing of the issuer's capability of repaying the obligation. This is why the credit ratings for unsecured forms of bonds only rely on the income source of the issuer in question.

Since the Global Financial Crisis destroyed the highest creditworthiness of many a long-standing AAA rated nation, neither the world's largest debtor nor creditor nations possess the all-important AAA rating. For example, S&P argues that it will only deliver the AAA rating in the cases where an "extremely strong capacity to meet financial commitments" exists.

The euro zone was long a shining example of many nations which possessed unanimous AAA rated credit. After the Great Recession and Sovereign Debt Crisis ravaged Europe, only the two nations of Luxembourg and Germany still retain this three ratings agency unanimous AAA status.

Acquisition

An acquisition refers to a corporate act where it purchases either controlling interest or complete interest in another company. Companies do this by buying out the stock shares in order to gain control of it. Technically, acquisitions happen as the buyer is able to acquire an over 50 percent ownership stake in the target firm. Typically the acquirer will buy all or many of the shares of the target's outstanding stock as well as assets. This allows them to make all decisions on the assets of the company they have taken over without needing any shareholder approval to proceed.

The buyer has several choices for how to pay for the acquisition. They can do it all in cash through buying out the target's shares, buy the company outright for cash, or use a combination of the two methods. The financial news is full of the mega merger and acquisition deals. As an example, Dow Chemical bought out DuPont in a $130 billion mega purchase back in 2015. Yet countless more medium sized to smaller businesses engage in merger and acquisition activity each and every year.

There are a number of reasons for why corporations engage in such acquisitions. It might be that they want to merge their enterprise with another for better economies of scale. This means that the costs of doing business, producing goods, and getting them to market decreases as a company becomes larger and does more volume in sales. They may desire to command a larger market share. It could be they foresee cost reductions and better synergy. Sometimes the acquirer wants a product, service, technology, research, or technical know-how that a target owns.

There are grander ambitions for acquisitions as well. Some domestic companies may want to grow their business into an international and eventually multinational corporate empire. Many times the only economically practical way (and the least expensive and simplest as well) to break into a foreign market is by simply buying out a company that is already operating successfully there.

This would be for the simple reasons that the target firm has a recognized brand name in the country, its own management and staff there, permission and licensing to operate there, and various intangible as well as physical assets in the country already. Besides this, the buyer will gain the solid customer base that the target has already established in the market.

Many times acquisitions will happen as a natural outgrowth of a firm's master strategy to increase its footprint in the business. The advantages to simply taking over already up and running operations versus starting new ones from scratch are considerable. Bigger corporations finally reach the stage where continuing to grow organically will cause them to decrease in operating efficiency. This can happen through too much bureaucracy as well as because of logistical or resource limitations. In such cases, the only viable means of gaining better growth and greater profits is through seizing hold of an aggressive young firm that it can simply fold into its own existing operations and revenue streams.

Another good reason for making acquisitions is because sometimes the competition in an industry becomes overcrowded. This can lead to overproduction of the goods in the company's line of business. Firms can utilize takeovers as a means of soaking up the overabundance of capacity through eliminating some competitors. It allows them to concentrate their operations on the greatest productivity providers as well.

A last good motivation for pursuing such acquisitions surrounds technology and know-how. Sometimes a new bit of technology becomes developed by a competitor. It may boost productivity yet cost a great amount of time and resources to develop internally. The most cost effective way of acquiring this technology is often in buying out the firm which already possesses or developed said technology. This saves the buyer the time, cost, and hassle of doing the research and development on their own.

Asset Backed Security (ABS)

An Asset Backed Security is also known by its acronym ABS. This refers to a type of financial security. These are commonly backed up using either a lease, a loan, or receivables against company assets (which would not include either mortgage backed securities or real estate). With the world of investing, such ABS provide other choices for those who wish to invest in something other than common corporate debt issues.

It is interesting to note that these Asset Backed Securities are more or less identical to MBS Mortgage Backed Securities. The primary difference lies in the securities which back the two financial instruments. With the ABS, they can include credit card debt, leases, loans, royalties, and even the receivables of the company issuing the debt. Yet these mortgage based securities may never underlie the ABS.

Such an Asset Backed Security delivers to the issuer of the security a means of creating more cash for the business. It allows yield hungry investors the chance to sink their money into a great range of assets which generate income. It is worth noting that most of these underlying assets will not be liquid. This means that they can not be readily sold as stand alone assets. Yet in pooling such assets into a single conglomeration, a financial security may be created. This is done in the process referred to as securitization. This permits the asset owner to employ them in a marketable fashion.

Among the assets of such pools could be car loans, home equity loans, student loans, credit card receivables, or other anticipated cash flow items. The capacity of Asset Backed Security issuers to be creative should never be underestimated. There have even been ABS which were established utilizing the cash flow generated by movie release revenues, aircraft leases, creative works and other forms of royalty payments, and even solar energy photovoltaic revenue streams. Practically any scenario where cash is produced can be packaged up via securitization into an ABS.

It is often helpful to consider an example of this somewhat complicated Asset Backed Security topic. Consider the case of a fictitious firm Car Loans For Everybody. When individuals wish to borrow funds to purchase a car, Car Loans For Everybody will issue them the cash in a check. The individual will have to pay back the loan along with a specified interest amount at a certain time in monthly installments. It could be that Car Loans is so successful at making automobile loans that they deplete their cash reserves and can no longer issue additional loans. They have the ability to sell off their present book of loans to the fictitious investment firm Imperial Legends. Imperial Legends will then provide them with the cash they need to continue issuing new loans.

This is only where the securitization process begins. Imperial Legends investment firm would then arrange the bought out loans into a collection of parcels known in the business as tranches. A tranche effectively is a batch of loans that posses similar features. This would include interest rates, maturity dates, and anticipated rates of delinquency. After this, the Imperial Legends firm would offer new securities with features much like bonds in every tranche they created.

Finally, investors will buy such securities. They obtain the underlying cash flow out of the pool of car loans, less the administration fee, which Imperial Legends will keep to cover their costs and towards their profit.

There are three typical types of tranches in an Asset Backed Security. These are commonly referred to as Class A, Class B, and Class C. Senior most tranches belong to Class A. They are generally the biggest tranche. They will be structured in such a way as to obtain a decent investment rating so that they are easily marketable to investors.

With the Class B tranche, the credit quality will necessarily be lower. This inversely means that the yield will be higher than that of the senior tranche. Since the risk is greater, investors need to be compensated for their appropriate risk of defaults.

Class C tranche has the lowest credit rating of all. It could be the credit quality is so poor that investors will refuse to consider it altogether. In such cases, the ABS issuer then holds the Class C tranche, collects the incoming revenues every month, and absorbs any losses themselves.

Balance Sheet

Balance Sheet refers to a corporate financial statement. The purpose of it is to thoroughly summarize the liabilities, assets, and shareholders' equity in the firm at a fixed moment in time. The statement provides a revealing glimpse into the things the corporation owns and the money it owes, along with the total amount which shareholders have invested in the going concern. Where these financial statements are concerned, the formula for assets is liabilities plus shareholders' equity.

Balance sheets ultimately derive their names from the equation which pits the assets on one side while the shareholders' equity and liabilities remain on the opposite site. They have to balance out, which provides the concept behind the name. It makes perfect sense that corporations have only two choices when paying for their assets. They might either borrow the money through assuming liabilities or obtain it off of investors, which happens when they issue shareholder equity.

Consider an example to better understand what is involved with this concept. If a corporation obtains a $40,000 bank loan to be repaid in five years, then its assets (cash account section) will rise by the $40,000. At the same time, the total liabilities (long term debt section) will also rise by the $40,000 amount. This restores balance to the equation. Should the firm then receive $80,000 from investors, the assets will also increase by that same amount. On the other side of the equation, the shareholder equity rises by the same $80,000. When the company earns revenues which are greater than the liabilities, these go into the so called shareholder equity account. It is that category that stands for all net assets the owners of the corporation hold. The offsetting revenues balance out on the assets side in the form of inventory, investments, or cash categories.

The three main categories of the balance sheet equation--- assets, liabilities, and shareholder equity each break down further into a few of their own sub accounts. These sub accounts actually reveal the particulars of the corporate finances. Every industry will have its own range of sub accounts. Many of the sub account terms will mean different things from one type of business to another. In general, there are always several sub account categories that different industries have in common.

As an example, under the assets category, such sub accounts are broken out from top down to bottom according to which is most liquid. This simply means the ease of selling them for cash. The divisions for all sub accounts will be by current assets and long term assets. The current ones may be changed to cash in under a year. Longer term ones obviously may not be converted so quickly. Current assets generally list top to bottom according to the following precedence: cash or cash equivalents, marketable securities, accounts receivable, inventory, and prepaid expenses. Longer term assets have the following general top down order: long term investments, fixed assets, and intangible assets such as goodwill, trademarks, and intellectual property.

Under the liabilities category will be the total amount firms owe to other entities. These include building rent, salaries, utilities, supplier invoices, and interest on loans or bonds. The current liabilities will be due in under a year, while the longer term ones are due after a year. Some sub accounts for current liabilities include: currently due part of longer term debt, interest payable, bank debts, wages payable, rents/utilities/taxes, dividend payments, and customer prepayments. Under longer term liabilities there are pension fund liabilities, long term debts, and deferred tax liabilities. There can also be off-balance sheet liabilities, like operating leases.

Shareholders' equity includes money from the owners of the business, the stake holding shareholders. This includes the net assets like treasury stock, retained earnings, preferred stock, and additionally paid in capital.

Balloon Loan

A balloon loan is a kind of loan that does not divide its payments up evenly throughout the life of the loan. These kinds of loans are not fully amortized over the loan's term. As a result of this, one time balloon payments are mandatory at the end of the loan's time frame in order to pay off the loan's remaining principal balance.

Balloon loans have their advantages. They are often appealing to you if you are a short term borrower. This is because balloon loans commonly come with an interest rate that is lower than the interest rate of a longer term loan. These lower interest rates provide a benefit of extremely low interest payments. This leads to not only lower payments throughout the loan, but also incredibly low outlays of capital in the life span of the loan. Because the majority of the loan repayment is put off until the loan payment period's conclusion, a borrower gains great flexibility in using the capital that is freed up for the term of the loan.

The downsides to these balloon loans only surface when the borrower lacks discipline or falls victim to higher interest rates later on. If a borrower does not possess focused and consistent discipline in getting ready for the large last payment, then the individual may run into trouble at the end of the loan. This is because substantial payments along the way are not being collected. Besides this, if a borrower will be forced to engage in refinancing towards the end, then the borrower may suffer from a higher interest rate on the balloon payment that is rolled forward.

Some balloon loans also include a higher interest rate reset feature later in the life of the loan. This further exposes a borrower to the risk of higher interest rates. This is common with five year types of balloon mortgages. When a reset of the interest rate feature is present at the conclusion of the five year period, then the interest rate will be adjusted to the current rates. The amortization schedule will then be recalculated dependent on a final term of the loan. Balloon options that do not include these reset options, and many that do reset, generally encourage the loan holder to sell the property in advance of the conclusion of the original term of the loan. Otherwise, many borrowers will simply choose to refinance the loan before this point arrives.

The reasons that you might choose to get a balloon loan are several. A person who does not plan to hold onto a house or property for a long period of time would benefit from such a loan arrangement. This individual would plan to resell the house in advance of the loan expiration. Another reason for taking a balloon loan is in a refinancing. Finally, if a person anticipates a significant cash settlement or lump sum award, then they might take on a balloon loan. Commercial property owners often like balloon loans for the purchase of commercial properties as well.

Balloon loans are sometimes called balloon notes or bullet loans.

Barclays

Barclays is a British based banking giant that calls its twin home markets both the United Kingdom and the United States. The bank is well known as a transatlantic consumer, investment, and corporate bank that provide financial services and products through investment, corporate, personal banking, wealth management, and credit cards. The banking group's goal is to concentrate on its core strengths in investment banking, consumer banking, and corporate banking from its two anchors in the financial capitals of the globe - London and New York City.

Barclays is the oldest of the major international global banks. Its history stretches back over 325 years to 1690 where it began on Lombard Street in London. Since then the bank has pioneered numerous first in banking achievements such as the first ATM machine in the globe to industry leading cell phone payment services.

The bank today operates in more than 40 countries and territories and maintains over 130,000 employees around the globe. It operates in such key international markets as the United States, Brazil, Canada, and Mexico in the Americas; Australia, India, China, Hong Kong, Indonesia, Malaysia, South Korea, Taiwan and Singapore in Asia Pacific; Egypt, Israel, Nigeria, South Africa, Kenya, Tanzania, and the UAE in Africa and the Middle East; and France, Germany, Italy, the Netherlands, Russia, Spain, Sweden, and Switzerland in Continental Europe.

The banking giant operates as two well defined and differentiated businesses. These are Barclays UK and Barclays Corporate & International. The bank's UK division caters to both consumers and small to medium sized businesses. This franchise has substantial scale throughout the United Kingdom. It is made up of their UK retail banking operations, the UK wealth offering, the UK consumer credit card business, and their corporate banking for smaller businesses.

This division counts 22 million individuals as retail customers and another one million business clients. This makes Barclays a leading financial products and services provider within the United Kingdom as well as the world. The bank will ring fence this division from its other operations by 2019 in an effort to protect traditional banking assets from other riskier endeavors of the investment bank.

Under Barclays UK, personal banking offers checking and savings accounts; personal, car, and credit card loans; travel, home, and life insurance; and mortgages. The UK credit cards business focus on the Barclay Card brand. Its wealth, entrepreneurs, and business banking business covers such offerings as private banking, wealth advisory, and wealth investment services.

Barclays Corporate & International division focuses on all of the rest of the bank's operations and offerings throughout the world. This diversified transatlantic banking division comprises their U.K. market leading corporate banking, world class investment bank, growing and powerful U.S. and global credit card businesses, international wealth services, and world leading merchant payments processing systems through Barclaycard merchant and corporate banking. The division boasts impressive size and scale in consumer lending and wholesale banking. It offers tremendous growth potential for the future, core strength in critical markets, and solid balance of revenue streams.

The bank's Corporate & International Division focuses on three key businesses. Its Corporate and Investment Bank provides big business banking, access to market securities and debt issue, and business research for its corporate clients. Consumer Cards and Payments concentrate on the proprietary Barclay Card credit card offering and merchant processing in the United States and overseas.

Barclaycard and Wealth International handles over 40 different credit card branding relationships, providing credit card services for travel, entertainment, educational, financial, and retail institutions. It also provides the wealth management services to the bank's many international individual and institutional clients.

Bear Stearns

Bear Stearns was formerly among the biggest important securities trading outfits within the United States. At one point it boasted a total asset base of almost $400 billion. The investment bank pursued a wide variety of financial activities. Among these were the clearing and trading of derivatives and securities, investment banking, brokerage account services, and creating and packaging up residential mortgages and commercial property loans.

In the swamping wake of the subprime mortgage meltdown and beginnings of the Global Financial Crisis, the company's financial condition rapidly and catastrophically deteriorated from the middle of January through the middle of March in 2008. March 13th was the day when Bear Stearns informed the Federal Reserve it would no longer have sufficient liquid cash-like assets or funds in order to cover its financial responsibilities the next day. It reported that there was no practical way it could come up with an alternative means of financing in time from the private sector.

The Federal Reserve considered that a looming insolvency of Bear Stearns the next day would create havoc in financial markets. This investment bank and brokerage was a dominant figure in a few different critical financial markets. Among these were especially the foreign exchange markets, over the counter derivative transactions, repo transactions, securities clearing services, and the market of mortgage backed securities.

The Fed considered that contagion from the failure of this systemically critical investment banking and market-making firm was highly likely. They feared that the day to day operations of the nation's (and even world's) financial markets would be severely compromised at the point where Stearns could not cover its various counterparty obligations. The Federal Reserve opted to provide credit so that the firm's affairs could be resolved in an orderly fashion.

The Federal Reserve considered the range of options and found they had grown thin. In order to deal with the urgent liquidity concerns Bear Stearns suffered from, they opted to have the FRBNY Federal Reserve Bank of New York extend $12.9 billion in credit via JP Morgan Chase Bank to Bears Stearns. This was necessary in order to delay systemic disruptions which the bankruptcy or at least default of the firm would have created in credit markets that were already highly stressed. The loan itself became secured by the $13.8 billion in market value assets which Stearns claimed on its balance sheet.

The entire reason of being for the bridge loan from the Federal Reserve Bank was to make certain the investment bank could cover its same-day and next-day obligations to counterparties. This would give it the weekend to consider what its options were and to discuss possibilities with the other major financial institutions that would make it possible to sidestep bankruptcy. It would also provide federal policy makers with some time to figure ways to limit the contagion to other financial institutions and markets if a private sector-based solution did not materialize in time.

On Monday, March 17th, the entire $12.9 billion emergency loan via JP Morgan Chase Bank to Stearns had been paid back to the Federal Reserve Bank of New York along with an almost $4 million in interest. Many critics at the time wondered how the Federal Reserve could pursue such an extraordinary measure as to provide credit to a member bank on such an enormous scale. The Fed cited Section 13(3) under the Federal Reserve Act. This allowed the Board itself to order Reserve Banks to provide credit to corporations, partnerships, or individuals in unusual and extraneous circumstances.

Despite the heroic efforts of the Federal Reserve to save Bear Stearns with its bridge loan, over the weekend the market pressure mounting against the company increased. It soon reached the point that it could not escape from bankruptcy by Monday, March 17th unless it received enormous liquidity injections from the Federal Reserve or an offer for acquisition by a larger, more financially sound financial institution. Fortunately for markets at that point, there was one such practical bidder in the form of JP Morgan Chase and Co. Bear Stearns agreed to merge with JPMC before markets reopened. This happened on Sunday, March 16th of 2008.

As part of the merger and because of the unknown scale of possible losses that Stearns faced from the stressed credit markets, the Fed had to help out with the transaction. The FRBNY was ordered to form a special Maiden Lane LLC to absorb the trading portfolio from Bear Stearns. It was this Fed holding company that purchased and gradually wound down around $30 billion worth of Bear Stearns assets utilizing a $29 billion loan from the

FRBNY and a $1 billion loan from JPMC.

Blanket Loans

Blanket loans are those which cover multiple properties or parcels of land. They handle the costs for or can be secured by more than a single piece of real estate. These are most typically employed by commercial land developers or investors. For individual consumers, they can be utilized as a type of bridge between new and old properties and mortgages. For these consumers, such a blanket loan will make it possible to pay for both mortgages until the owner reaches the point of selling the old property.

The feature that makes these mortgages most useful for developers is their release clause. These permit the borrowers to sell a single or even several pieces of real estate without the need of being forced to refinance the mortgage. This makes them significantly different from traditional mortgages. Normal mortgages make borrowers completely pay down their loan balance before they can sell the property which secures them.

For developers of residential properties, they find these blanket loans particularly helpful. They employ them to pay for large tracts of land on which they will build. When it is time for the loan to fund, it becomes secured by the full piece of property. The developer is allowed to subdivide his property and sell it in individual lots. For part of the security to be released, the developer must utilize some of the sale proceeds to pay down part of the loan.

This is helpful when builders are constructing subdivisions. Such a developer could put the blanket loan to use to buy the consecutive pieces of land while they are available. The developer would then be able to subdivide the total land into specific lots for building houses. With each home that he finishes and sells, the property becomes detached from the blanket loan without the financing having to be disrupted on the remainder of the development project.

Consumers also find these types of blanket loans helpful in making it possible to transition from the sale of their current home to the building or buying of the new house. This makes much more sense than having two concurrent mortgages or obtaining a more costly short term bridge loan. It can also help them so that they do not have to sell the property early and move into a rental while they look for a property to purchase.

These kinds of blanket loans are often governed by a contingency clause. These clauses detail that the newly purchased house and its mortgage will not close until the person is able to sell the existing home. The problem with such a contingency clause is that they have limited time frames on them. They may force a borrower into selling the home in a panic in order to meet the clause expiration date. This can lead to a lower selling price or disadvantageous terms on the sale.

Blanket loans get around such a dilemma by providing the borrowers with an extended period of time in the clause to sell their old house. Sometimes they are arranged as interest payment only loans for a full 12 months before amortizing starts. This gives the seller a sufficient time period to sell the house for a good price and reduces the overall burden of the mortgage at the same time.

The main downside to blanket loans for individuals is that they are significantly harder to find since the real estate crash and Great Recession of 2009. Their advantages include both flexibility and efficiency in financing. For an individual consumer, this means a single mortgage payment rather than two. Developers do not have to worry about constantly refinancing their property debt as they sell off parts of the property. Should a developer default on his loan, the bank simply assumes control of all remaining property which secures the loan.

BNP Paribas

BNP Paribas is the largest French-based bank in the world. It has strong roots in the banking history of Europe. Today it remains one of the leading banks on the continent and Euro zone as well as an important international banking group. The group claims 189,000 employees around the world, of which the overwhelming majority of 146,610 are based in Europe.

It also has an extensive international network of branches and employees. The bank maintains 19,845 employees in America; 12,180 workers in Asia; 9,860 staff members in Africa; and 580 employees in the Middle East, as of 2015. BNP Paribas locations can be found in 75 different countries and territories around the world. For 2015, it boasted 42.9 billion euros of revenue and 6.7 billion euros of net profit.

The bank organizes itself along two main business lines. These are Retail Banking and Services (RBS) and the Corporate Institutional Banking (CIB) divisions. The Retail Banking & Services division covers its retail banking activities and specialized financial products and services in both France and the rest of the world. The company subdivides this into Domestic Markets and International Financial Services.

The group's Domestic Markets is comprised of the company's four retail banking networks found in the euro zone, as well as three specific lines of business. The retail bank networks are FRB French Retail Banking located in France, BNP Paribas Fortis in Belgium, BNL in Italy, and BGL BNP Paribas found in Luxembourg. Its three specific business lines are Arval the long term corporate leasing program, its Leasing Solutions that provide financing and rental services, and its Personal Investors that offer online brokerage services and savings vehicles.

Corporate clients also can access the business of Cash Management and Factoring. High Net Worth Individuals have the company's Wealth Management business as their private banking franchise within the domestic markets of the group. As of 2015, the Domestic Markets subdivision boasts over 15 million individual customers located in 27 countries. The bank also counts almost 1 million clients comprised of professional individuals, small businesses, and corporate entities. To service these numerous accounts, they devote the efforts of 68,000 employees in these over two dozen countries.

International Financial Services of the group handles the company's diversified business activities operating in over 60 countries. The group's Personal Finance provides credit to people residing in 30 countries. They deliver products and services via such major brands as Findomestic, Cofinoga, and Cetelem.

The IFS division also operates several other businesses. International Retail Banking covers the retail bank operations in another 15 non-euro zone nations like TEB in Turkey and Bank of the West in the U.S. BNP Paribas Cardif offers savings and insurance for assets, projects, and individuals living in 36 countries.

IFS rounds out its business lines with three specific asset management and private banking operations. These include the group's Wealth Management for private banking, their Investment Partners for asset management, and their BNP Paribas Real Estate for international real estate services. All of the International Financial Services businesses and lines together employ over 80,000 staff residing in over 60 countries.

The group's Corporate & Institutional Banking (CIB) prides itself on being a leading worldwide provider of financial products and services to its institutional and corporate clients around the globe. They group counts 13,000 of these clients in 57 countries throughout Europe/Middle East/Africa, the America, and Asia Pacific. To support them it maintains nearly 30,000 staff.

The company delivers specialized services that help their clients through treasury, financing, securities services, capital markets, and financial advisory offerings. It proves to be a world-renowned leader throughout numerous disciplines. As such, CIB has vast expertise in derivatives, risk management, structured financing, and other areas. The CIB division serves as a bridge between the two types of clients it counts by helping its corporate clients to obtain financing while offering investment possibilities to its institutional investors.

Bond Market

A bond market is a financial market where investors buy and sell bonds. In practice this is mostly handled electronically over computers nowadays. There are two principal types of bond markets. These are primary markets where companies are able to sell new debt and secondary markets where investors are able to purchase and resell these debt securities. Companies generally issues such debt as bonds. These markets also trade bills, notes, and commercial paper.

The goal of the bond markets is to help private companies and public entities obtain funding of a long term nature. This market has generally been the domain of the United States that dominates it. The U.S. comprises as much as 44% of this bond market on a global basis.

There are five primary bond markets according to SIFMA the Securities Industry and Financial Markets Association. These include the municipal, corporate, mortgage or asset backed, funding, and government or agency markets. The government bond market comprises a significant component of this market thanks to its massive liquidity and enormous size. Because of the stability of U.S. and some international government bonds, other bonds are often contrasted with them to help determine the amount of credit risk.

This is because government bond yields from countries with little risk like the U.S., Britain, or Germany are traditionally considered to be free of default risk. Other bonds denominated in these various currencies provide greater yields as the borrowers are more likely to default than these central governments.

Bond markets often serve a useful secondary function to reveal interest rate changes. This is because the values of bonds are inversely related to the interest rates which they pay. This helps investors to measure what the true cost of obtaining funding really is. Companies which are perceived to be riskier will have to pay higher interest rates on their bonds than companies believed to have strong and stable credit and repayment abilities. When companies or government entities are unable to make a partial or full payment on their bonds, this becomes a default.

When a company or a government needs to raise money and does not want to issue stock, it can sell bonds. These are contracts the issuers who are the borrowers make with investors who function as lenders. When investors purchase such instruments, they lend money to the issuing organization (company or government). The issuer of the bond promises to repay the original investment back along with interest in the future.

Bonds traded on these markets have many elements in common, whichever type of market they represent. All bonds have a face value. This is the amount of money which a bond would be valued at when it matures and the amount on which interest payments are based. They also have coupon rates that represent the interest rate which the issuer of the bond pays in its interest payments.

The coupon dates turn out to be the times when the issuer will pay its interest payments. Issue prices are the amounts for which the issuer sells the bond in the first place. The maturity date proves to be the exact date when the bond would be repaid. At this time, the issuer of the bond would pay the bond's face value to the bond holder.

Though a holder of a bond might keep it until maturity, this is often not the case. Many investors buy and sell them on the bond markets as their needs dictate. It is possible to sell a bond at a premium when the market value becomes greater than the original face value. Investors could also sell them at a discount to their original face value as the market price declines.

Cap Rate

Cap rate refers to the real estate property and its rate of return. Investors figure this out by utilizing the income which they anticipate the property will generate. The cap rate is also referred to as the capitalization rate. Realtors utilize it to gauge how much return investors will realize on their investments.

The way people determine this cap rate is by using an easy to understand formula. Investors take the property's NOI net operating income and divide it by the current fair market value of the property. This NOI turns out to be the annual return less all operating costs. The capitalization rate formula can be written as Capitalization Rate = Net Operating Income / Current Market Value. Investors and realtors express it as a percentage.

Investors consider the cap rate to be very helpful because it summarizes information regarding real estate investments. It is also simple to understand. This important rate discerns the profitability of a given piece of property. In order for it to remain consistent, the net operating income and current market value have to be constant compared to each other. If the NOI goes up when market value remains constant, the capitalization rate rises. If instead market value increases while NOI remains the same, then this rate will go down.

Real estate investments only stay profitable if the NOI goes up at the same rate as or a greater rate than the increase in the value of the property. This is another way that the capitalization rate is helpful. It can be employed to track the performance of real estate investments through time to learn if their performance is increasing. When the rate declines instead, investors may decide to sell the property so that they can reinvest the capital in some other place.

The cap rate is especially practical because it allows individuals to measure different investments in property. It permits them to compare and contrast a number of different investment possibilities against each other. Sometimes it is not easy to compare operating income or market values of radically different properties. Comparing percentages to one another is simple and intuitive. The rate is at its most useful when either the current market value or NOI are similar. This is because investments where the cost is vastly different can create a variety of other considerations that interfere with effective comparison.

Many times investors will come up with a minimum capitalization rate which they are willing to take so that the investment is practical. They might set 12% as their minimum rate. This helps them to sift through the various possibilities to rule out the ones that do not measure up to their desired minimum.

Investors may also employ the capitalization rate to figure out the amount of time it will take for the investment to reach its payback point. They can find the payback period by taking 100 and dividing it by the capitalization rate. This will provide an estimate of the payback period and not a fixed number. Most investments will see their capitalization rate change during significant amounts of time.

Another useful way of determining the value for a real estate investment is to utilize direct capitalization. To find this number, investors simply divide their NOI by the cap rate. This provides them with the capital cost of the real estate investment in question.

Investors should realize that the capitalization rate is not so helpful for shorter time frame investments as it is for longer ones. Figuring up NOI requires some time to determine a cash flow number that is reliable.

Capital Expenditures

Capital expenditure refers to money that a firm employs to purchase physical assets. This can also be used to upgrade existing assets. These can include items such as equipment, industrial buildings, and property. It is also known as CapEx. Companies often use this CapEx to make new investments or to begin a new project.

Other corporations utilize capital expenditures to build up their operations' size and scale. Such expenditures can cover many different items like buying a new piece of equipment, fixing the roof on a company building, or constructing a new factory for the company.

Accounting procedures utilize this capital expenditure concept regularly. Expenses will be labeled as CapEx if the item the company buys is a new purchase of a capital asset. They also fall under this category when the purchase is some type of investment that extends the practical life of an already owned capital asset.

When a purchase falls under the capital expenditure's category, the accounting department will be required to capitalize it. They do this when the fixed cost of the purchase is spread out over the asset's useful life. In other cases, the money they spend will only keep the capital item in its present condition. For these scenarios the company and accountants may simply deduct the entire expense for the year in which they spend the money.

Different industries will employ varying levels of capital expenditures. Some use very little, while others are more capital intensive. Among the most intensive capital industries in the world are the exploration and production of energy such as oil or natural gas, manufacturing businesses, telecommunications, and electricity, gas, and water utilities.

It is important to not confuse capital expenditures with other ideas like operating expenses, known as OPEX, or revenue expenditures. Operating and revenue expenses are money that companies pay to cover the daily cost of running the business. Revenue expenses are different from CapEx in another significant way. The former can be completely deducted from taxes in the year in which the company spends them.

Capital expenditures can be used to help come up with the relative value of a company also. Cash flow to capital expenditure ratio is one such measure. It is commonly referred to as CF/CapEx. This explains the ability of a company to purchase assets for long term use by utilizing its free cash flow. This ratio commonly goes up and down for businesses as they engage in cycles of small capital versus large capital expenses.

Ideally a business wants to have a higher multiple in this ratio. Higher numbers signify that the company is in a position of solid financial health and strength. This is because firms that possess the financial capabilities to invest in their future with capital expenditures can expand with greater ease and flexibility.

Cash flows to capital expenditures are ratios that are specific to every industry. Each segment's ratio will be different. This means that the ratio of one company in one business should not be compared to a second company in another industry. Instead, the ratio is only useful for comparison when two companies that possess comparable CapEx requirements are examined. Comparing various CapEx ratios from two oil firms or utility companies makes sense. Holding up the CapEx ratios of an oil company or telecom firm against a consulting business or advertising agency does not.

The higher a company's capital expenditure is, the lower its other measures of financial health may be. As an example, firms with high CapEx will often show less free cash flow to equity.

Capital Markets

Capital markets refer to those marketplaces for the sales and purchase of both debt and equity financial issues. These markets move investments and savings back and forth between capital suppliers like institutional and retail investors to capital users. These are individual entrepreneurs, businesses and corporations, and governmental agencies. Economies do not function efficiently or successfully without such liquid markets of capital. This is because capital is a crucial component for producing economic output.

There are two types of such capital markets. These include the primary markets and secondary markets. In the primary markets, investors buy and sell new bond and stock instruments. Secondary markets are the ones that trade already existing securities. The two financial instruments categories are equities and debt securities. The equities are typically called stocks. The debt securities are usually called bonds. Such markets revolve around the selling of bonds and stocks for longer and medium term durations, typically of at least a year.

These capital markets in the United States function under the auspices of the Securities and Exchange Commission. In other nations, they operate under different financial regulators. In general, such markets tend to cluster in the several important financial centers of the globe. The greatest of these are London, New York City, Hong Kong, and Singapore. Despite the fact that the markets lie in these principal city centers, the majority of their trades happen via sophisticated electronic and computer trading systems. While members of the public can access some such capital centers in person, the other ones remain highly secured and regulated.

Primary markets are where these investments first appear. The companies which need to raise capital issue bonds and stocks directly to the financial institutions, businesses, and investors here. They typically buy these in a process called underwriting. Another advantage offered by companies which require capital is that they can do it there without having to hold initial public offerings (IPOs) so that the profit remains theirs. When companies do opt for IPOs, they typically sell all of their stock shares off to several underwriting investment banks through a lead investment bank and other financial firms which choose to participate.

From this stage, the new shares become a part of the secondary market. Here the investment banks, financial firms, and private investors are allowed to resell their debt and equity instruments to retail investors.

There are many entities which participate in capital markets. These include institutional investors like mutual funds and pension funds, retail investors, corporations and other organizations, governments and municipalities, and financial institutions and banks. Governments may be allowed to issue bonds on these markets, but they can never sell equity via stocks.

These markets are where supply and demand between capital suppliers and users meet and adjust. While capital users desire to raise their capital for the lowest cost they possibly can, the suppliers wish to obtain the highest return they possibly can for the least amount of risk possible.

A country's capital markets' size will be directly proportional to the economic size of the nation in question. As the biggest economy on the planet, the U.S. boasts the deepest and biggest capital markets. These markets are still interdependent on other such capital centers in the global economy of today. Small ripples in another center such as London or Hong Kong can lead to substantial waves in Singapore and/or New York City.

The downside to the interconnectedness of the financial and capital centers is illustrated by the financial and credit crisis of 2007 to 2009. It was actually the failure of the mortgage-backed securities markets in the United States that triggered the crisis and collapse. This de facto meltdown in the U.S. became transmitted around the world by the global capital markets as financial institutions, investment banks, and commercial banks throughout both Europe and Asia were holding literally trillions of U.S. dollars worth of such securities.

Capital Stock

A business' capital stock is the up front capital that the founders of the firm invest in or put into the company. This capital stock also proves useful as security for a business' creditors. This is because capital stock may not be taken out of the business to disadvantage the creditors in question. Such stock is separate from a business' assets or property that can rise and fall in value and amount.

A company's capital stock is segregated into shares. The complete number of such shares have to be detailed when the business is founded. Based on the entire sum of money that is put into the company when it is started up, each share will possess a particular face value that must be declared.

This value is referred to as par value of the individual shares. These par values are the minimum sums of money that may be issued and sold in stock shares by the business. It is similarly the capital value representation in the business' own accounting. In some countries, these shares do not contain any par value period. In this case, the capital stock shares would be termed non par value stock. Such shares literally represent a portion of an ownership in the business in question. These businesses may then declare various classes of shares. All of these could have their own privileges, rules, and share values.

The owning of such capital stock shares is proven by the possession of a certificate of stock. These stock certificates prove to be legal documents that detail the numbers of shares each shareholder owns. Other particular data of the capital stock shares, including class of shares and par value, is similarly detailed on these certificates.

These owners of the firm in question may decide that they need more capital in order to invest in additional projects that the company has in mind. Besides this, they might decide that they want to cash out some of their own holdings in order to release a portion of capital for their own private needs. They can do this by selling all or some of their capital stock to many partial owners. The ownership of one such share gives the share owner an ownership stake in the company. This includes such privileges as a tiny portion of any profits that may be paid out as dividends, as well as a small part of any decision making powers.

These shares sold from the capital stock each represent a single vote. The owners could decide to offer various classes of shares that could then have differing rights of voting. By owning a majority of the shares, the owners can out vote all of the little shareholders combined. This permits the original owners to maintain effective control of their company even after issuing shares of their capital stock to investors.

Cash Management

Cash management refers to the corporate functions of gathering, handling, and short term investing cash. This represents a critical part of making certain a firm is financially viable and stays solvent. In many cases, the business managers of a company or corporate treasurers of a large corporation will handle the aggregate cash management responsibilities. This means they will be responsible for ensuring the firm continues to be financially viable and solvent on a week to week basis.

There is more to successfully handled cash management than simply sidestepping financial problems or even bankruptcy. This job also involves bringing in invoice payments and account receivables, boosting the rates and speed of collection, improving the level of available cash at hand, and picking out relevant short term investment instruments which will all contribute to better profits and a stronger cash position for the firm in question.

Those small business managers and developers must learn to manage cash flow well since they do not enjoy low cost access to easy credit. They also encounter many ongoing running costs that they have to stay on top of while they are waiting for their customers to pay their receivables. By properly and prudently managing their cash flow, firms are able to cover unanticipated costs and to effectively cover their routine financial events like payroll on a bi-weekly or semi-monthly basis. The point of cash management is to effectively balance out two main corporate counteracting forces. These are the receivables for incoming cash and the outflows of payables.

Part of the dilemma for many companies struggling to effectively run their cash management operations is that invoices and receivables are positive cash flow on the books, yet in practice they are not always received immediately. Some invoice terms allow for the customer to wait from 30 to 60 to even 90 days to settle their invoices. This is how businesses can actually find themselves in the uncomfortable position of their sales growing even rapidly and still have cash flow problems because their receivables come in slowly or even unfortunately late.

Businesses have a variety of tools and means to speed up their receivables so that their payment float becomes reduced. Some of these are to deploy an auto billing service that immediately invoices the customers electronically, to make clear the billing and payment terms to the clients, to keep on top of all collections with an aging receivables spreadsheet, to offer incentives for same as cash 10 day invoice payments, and to collect payments via electronic payment processing at a bank.

Businesses which are successful in controlling their payables will be better capable of maintaining positive cash flows. Through streamlining the efficiency of the payables operations, firms are able to lower their costs all the while holding on to more cash which they can put to work in the company operations. There are a wide variety of effective payable management solutions available today. Some of these include direct payroll deposits, payment processing which is handled electronically, and closely and carefully controlled cash disbursements. Each of these processes will help to both automate and make efficient all of the payout operations.

Thanks to the variety of digital age offerings, the vast majority of payable management and receivable operations may be simply automated through current day solutions in business banking. Smaller companies are now able to operate with the same big scale technologies for cash management as the mega corporations. This is in no small part due to the rapid march of technological advances across business solutions and banking. Such cost savings created by these cutting-edged cash management techniques effectively more than offset the costs of utilizing them. The best part of the process nowadays is that a firm's management is capable of allocating critical resources to expanding the core business better than ever before possible.

Cash Operating Cost

Cash Operating Cost refers to a cash flow statement which effectively follows all cash types of business expenditures. It is in the first section of a cash flow statement, the operating activities, that keeps all relevant and pertinent information regarding the cash operating costs. Such expenses are derived from the firm's information on financial accounting. It does not matter if the expense items are variable or fixed.

The cash flow statement merely details the quantity of such cash operating costs as well as if the firm had a cash outflow or inflow over a particular time frame. This section covers a variety of cash expenditures. Among these are payables, assets, and various other current liabilities.

Payables are those things that corporations buy on account. They promise to pay the vendor later on in the arrangement. There are a wide variety of items which will be detailed in this section. Among them are wages, notes, interest, payroll, and any taxes due. Cash utilization happens as a company pays off the prior balance on any such items in the current month period. There will be a single line that refers to the repayment of these types of liabilities in the cash operating costs. Payables accounts increasing mean that cash flow for the firm is decreasing to match. This is because these are money the company has spent.

Assets prove to be among the most significant category of these cash operating costs. This is particularly the case with retail and manufacturing businesses that will be heavy on assets especially. Such assets detailed out here would include inventory, prepaid assets, supplies, accounts receivable, and other forms of current assets. Such items are typically utilized in the day to day business operations. The anticipation is that the various individual groups will not last for over 12 months. For these, the statement of cash flows shows real money which the firm pays for such items. Each particular category will have its own line on the statement along with the aggregate amount the category spend in a particular time frame.

The categories of other current liabilities will be a last section of the cash operating costs. Such items can be revenue that is unearned or various other current liabilities which firms incur in the normal course of business operations. Every item which does not adhere to the above two criterion will be listed out by the accountants in this category section. This includes special and one time items. It allows for the company accountant to make shareholders aware of substantial types of expenses which the normal business operations are costing. Sometime special disclosures will be required to be made to the various stock holders when major cash position reductions occur as a result of them.

Such statements of cash flow are useful for external and internal stake holders in a given corporation alike. The company accountants can also put together various other types of reports to show the cash operating costs for the firm. Such reports would be less formal yet still official. They explain the relevant cost items for the internal stakeholders such as upper level management and the board of directors. So long as the accountant utilize standard accounting processes, any range of statistics and figures could be included in the informational reports. In these cases, they may use whatever format they wish to produce the additional illuminating report.

Cash Reserves

Cash reserves refer to money which an individual person, a company, or a corporation saves in order to be ready to cover any emergency funding or short term requirements. They can also be utilized to refer to a kind of extremely liquid, short term investment which usually garners a poor rate of return (under three percent in a year).

An example of this would be Fidelity Cash Reserves, one of the Fidelity mutual families of funds particular investments. Sometimes individuals will hold money they need rapid access to in such a fund which can be instantly liquidated on the same day they issue the order. Possessing a major amount in a cash reserve fund provides corporations, companies, individuals, families, or communities with the necessary capability to engage in a significant purchase right away.

There are various reasons why firms wish to maintain some cash reserves. They need to have sufficient money on hand in order to cover all of their costs which may be anticipated or even unanticipated over the short term time-frame. Besides this, they often prefer to have enough cash readily available for such interesting possible investments which could arise with little to no warning.

Though cash is always considered to be the most liquid type of wealth and assets, there are also short term kinds of assets like three month U.S. Treasury bills which investors also deem to be a type of a cash reserve because of the ease and frequency with which they can exchange them and their close proximity to maturity date. Major corporations like Alphabet (Google), General Electric, IBM, and Apple keep enormous cash reserves available. These typically range from fifty billion dollars to one hundred and fifty billion dollars.

At the beginning of 2016, Apple boasted such cash reserve ranging from fifty billion to one hundred fifty billion dollars. At the same time, Alphabet (Google) counted $75.3 billion in their immediate cash on hand reserves. This permitted Google to buy out major corporate purchases like their acquisition of Nest, which they bought for a hefty $3 billion price tag back in 2014.

With banks, governmental oversight agencies require that they maintain a minimum quantity of cash reserves on hand. This is because their operations are critical for the functioning of any economy. In the United States, it is the American Federal Reserve that determines these cash reserve amounts for the banks. In other countries, it is often the national central bank or some other governmental oversight regulator who makes the call.

Banking cash reserves will typically be set as a certain percentage of the banks' liabilities or net transaction accounts. With those banks which contain in excess of $110.2 million in their net transaction accounts, this amount within the U.S. proves to be 10 percent of such liabilities. This amount became effective on January 1st of 2016. Such bank reserves have to be kept in either deposits at a Federal Reserve Bank or in their own vaults as cash on hand. With euro currency liabilities or time deposits of a non-personal nature, these liabilities are not subjected to such a cash reserve requirement.

Economists and personal finance gurus generally state that individuals are wise to keep minimally sufficient cash on hand to cover from three to six months of expenses in the event they suffer a family emergency. Such an emergency fund is a form of a cash reserve. These reserves would be kept in either their local bank accounts or otherwise in a stable and short term time frame investment which will maintain its value regardless of what happens in the markets. In this way, individuals are able to draw on their own emergency funds or alternatively to sell such investments at a moment's notice without taking a financial loss. This needs to be the case no matter how the financial investment markets are performing.

Other forms of personal cash reserves could be held in a savings account, checking account, money market account, money market fund, or even CDs and Treasury Bills. For those businesses or individuals who do not plan ahead with enough cash reserves, they may have to instead to fall back on credit, loans, or in some drastic cases, declaring bankruptcy.

Chapter 11 Bankruptcy

Chapter 11 Bankruptcy proves to be a specific type of bankruptcy. This kind has to do with the business assets, debts, and affairs being reorganized. The business reorganization filing was named for the Section 11 of the United States' Bankruptcy Code. Corporations commonly file it that need some time to rearrange the terms of their debts and their business operations. It gives them a fresh start on repaying their debt obligations. Naturally the indebted company will have to stick to the terms of the reorganization plan. This proves to be the most highly complex type of bankruptcy filing possible. Companies have been advised to only entertain it once they have contemplated their other options and analyzed the repercussions of such a filing.

This Chapter 11 bankruptcy rarely makes the news unless it is a nationally known or famous corporation which is filing. Among the major corporations that have filed such a Chapter 11 bankruptcy are United Airlines, General Motors, K-Mart, and Lehman Brothers. The first three successfully emerged from it and became as great or stronger than they were before falling into hard times financially. In reality, the vast majority of these cases are unknown to the general public. As an example, in the year 2010, nearly 14,000 separate corporations filed for Chapter 11.

The point of this Chapter 11 Bankruptcy is to assist a corporation in restructuring both obligations and debts. The goal is not to close down the business. In fact it rarely leads to the corporation closing. Instead, corporations like K-mart, General Motors, and tens of thousands of others were able to survive and once again thrive thanks to the useful process of protection from creditors and reorganization of business debts.

It is typically LLCs Limited Liability Companies, partnerships, and corporations that make application for Chapter 11 Bankruptcy. There are cases where individuals who are positively saddled with debt and who are not able to be approved for a Chapter 13 or Chapter 7 filing can be qualified for Chapter 11 instead. The time table for successfully completing Chapter 11 bankruptcy ranges from several months to as long as two years.

Businesses that are in the middle of their Chapter 11 cases are encouraged to keep operating. The debtor in possession will typically run the business normally. Where there are cases that have gross incompetence, dishonest dealings, or even fraud involved, typically trustees come in to take over the business and its daily operations while the bankruptcy proceedings are ongoing.

Corporations in the midst of these filings will not be permitted to engage in specific decisions without first having to consult with the courts to proceed. They may not terminate or sign rental agreements, sell any assets beyond regular inventory, or expand existing business operations or alternatively cease them. The bankruptcy court retains full control regarding any hiring and paying of lawyers as well as signing contracts with either unions or vendors. Lastly, such indebted organizations and entities may not sign for a loan that will pay once the bankruptcy process finishes.

After the business or person files their chapter 11 bankruptcy, it gains the right to offer a first reorganization plan. Such plans often include renegotiating owed debts and reducing the company size in order to slash expenses. There are some scenarios where the plan will require every asset to be liquidated in order to pay off the creditors, as with Lehman Brothers.

When plans are fair and workable, courts will approve them. This moves the reorganization process ahead. For plans to be accepted, they also have to maintain the creditors' best interests for the future repayment of debts owed to them. When the debtor can not or will not put forward a plan of their own for reorganization, then the creditors are invited to offer one in the indebted company or person's place.

Charge Off

A charge off refers to an expense item found on a corporation's income statement. This could be one of two things. It might be connected with a debt that the reporting firm has decided is not realistically collectable. They would then write this off from the corporate balance sheet. It might also be a likely one time only expense which is called an extraordinary event. The company incurs this, and it impacts the earnings negatively. This then leads to a portion of the corporate assets' becoming written down in value. Because the assets have become impaired, the write down occurs.

Where bad debt costs crop up, this is related to a company not being able to collects bills owed for at least a portion of its accounts receivable, also called AR. These events unfortunately happen sometimes, and firms can do little about them. They might attempt to sell off the likely bad debts to an interested collection agency. The company would then record a sale on the books, yet it would not be marked down as an expense item. Otherwise, they might simply charge off the amount which is uncollectable on the income statement by calling it an expense.

In order for debts to be considered to be bad debts, they have to be run up in the typical operations of the business. Such a debt could be incurred by either a person or another company. These charge offs for the bad debts more typically happen as companies extend credit (to other entities) that is unsecured. Examples of this would be signature-only loans or credit cards.

One time expenses which are charged off are another story altogether. Sometimes a firm will consent to an extraordinary charge off in a given period of accounting. This would impact the current period earnings, yet they feel it will not likely happen again in the near future. The end result is ultimately that the company will commonly offer its EPS earnings per share numbers both without and with the charge off in question reflected. This allows them to show the company shareholders that the expense is unusual and uncommon. They might also call this a one off charge.

Such charge offs could involve the buying of a major asset. This could be a significant piece of equipment or a brand new production facility. These expenses would not be repeated too often. There might also be charges that are associated with an unusual event. Examples of this are paying deductibles for insured items that became damaged in a natural disaster. There could also be a flood or a fire for which the firm has to pay the costs to cover the damage.

There might also be maintenance types of expenses that are not normal. These might include replacing a roof. It is true that maintenance issues like these can be predicted to a degree. Because the exact date of service and amount of charge can not easily be quantified. Since such maintenance issues are only necessary every few decades, they are extraordinary items indeed.

Charge offs could also pertain to individuals who have seen one of their personal debts charged off. Such an event does not mean that a creditor has specifically cancelled the debt. Borrowers will still have to pay off the balance in theory. When credit card payments become late, they go into late payment status. After a payment is 180 days late, the creditor companies will at last charge off the debt. They might then send it out for collection agencies or file lawsuits if the laws of the state where the debtor resides allow.

Citigroup

By number of countries and territories in which it operates as well as raw numbers of customers, Citigroup is the largest global bank. The United States based banking giant offers a substantial variety of financial products and services to its 100 million individual, corporate, institutional, and government customers around the world. The bank maintains a presence in more than 100 countries and territories throughout the globe. It operates in two primary groups of the Global Consumer Bank and the Institutional Clients Group.

Citigroup's Global Consumer Bank offers services throughout the most rapidly expanding cities in 24 different countries around the world. This group boasts over 100 million individual customers. Within the Global Consumer Bank (GCB), Citi runs four geographically based business lines in their four regions of North America, Latin America, Asia, and Europe/Middle East/Africa.

These are Retail Banking, Commercial Banking, Retail Services, and Branded Credit Cards. The Citi GCB boasts over a century of well-respected market leadership and brand recognition throughout areas such as the United States, Mexico, and Asia. It is focused on expanding its high credit profiled customer base utilizing its global abilities and reach.

The Institutional Clients Group operates in over 100 countries. It is here that Citigroup is able to assist multinational corporations in expanding, hiring, providing services, and delivering products. Citi proudly offers finance capabilities and support to not only companies, but also governments at every level. It assists them not only in funding their daily operations, but also in creating sustainable transportation, housing, infrastructure, schools, and other key public works and services.

Institutional investors are able to maximize the depth of product offerings and global footprint to reach into both local and international markets. Citigroup boasts an impressive history of financing among the most transforming projects in the world during the last two centuries. They remain devoted to supporting expansion and creative innovation around the world today with cash management, lending, and advisory services.

The Citigroup ICG maintains trading floors in over 80 nations, as well as custody and clearing networks in more than 60 countries and has connections via 400 different clearing systems. This means that Citi proudly controls among the biggest global financial facilities and infrastructure platforms. These help it to facilitate the movement of a daily average of more than $3 trillion in global monetary flows.

The ICG Group if Citigroup operates six primary businesses. Citi's Capital Markets Origination business concentrates on raising capital for their institutional clients. This includes cross border issues, transactions, and exchanges.

The Citigroup Corporate and Investment Banking business delivers complete relationship coverage and service utilizing product, sector, and nation expertise to provide their worldwide abilities to clients in whichever market they wish to have a competitive presence. They organize these teams by country and industry. Every team is comprised of the two parts. Strategic Coverage Officers provides for merger and acquisition and equity financing activities. Corporate Bankers work with the Global Subsidiaries Group and Citi Capital Markets in order to help provide finance and banking services to local, national, regional, and global customers.

Citi's Markets and Securities Services business delivers world-leading financial services and products to its thousands of institutions, investors, corporations, and government clients. It covers an impressive array of asset classes, sectors, currencies, and products. Among these products are commodities, equities, futures, credit, emerging markets, foreign exchange, G10 rates, prime finance, municipals, and securitized markets.

The Citigroup Global Private Bank business is a world leader. They have 800 private bankers residing in 16 countries at 51 individual offices who provide dependable advice to members of the most successful families and influential private individuals on earth.

Finally, the Citigroup Treasury and Trade Solutions, or TTS, business delivers trade finance and seamless cash management services to Citi's wide range of financial institutions, multinational corporations, and public sector outfits throughout the world. These services include receivables, payments, investment services, liquidity management services, commercial card programs, working capital solutions, and trade finance.

Collaboration

Collaboration proves to be a process where two or more individuals or entities choose to work in concert on behalf of a common goal or endeavor. Intellectual enterprises and other activities that tend to be creative by their nature are often most effectively accomplished through collaboration, which involves learning together, mutually sharing knowledge, and building up consensus. Scientific collaboration is very common because of this.

Most forms of collaboration must have leadership. Such leadership does not have to be in the form of traditional command structures, but can instead be social leadership affected in a group of equals or alternatively that is decentralized. Reasons for practicing collaboration are fairly evident. Teams working together in collaboration have access to a greater number of resources, rewards, and recognition when they compete for limited resources.

Collaboration can be extremely structured. When it is set up like this, then inward looking communication and behavior are encouraged. Such forms of collaboration particularly attempt to boost teams' successes as they work on problem solving in collaboration. Charts, graphs, rubrics, and forms are all utilized in this type of collaboration in order to lay out personalities and personal characteristics without bias, so that the future and present projects' collaboration will be bettered.

In business and finance, collaboration can be as simple as a partnership or as complicated as a multinational corporation. Team members that work together in an organization using collaboration achieve superior communication both in the business supply chains and the entire outfit. Such collaboration proves to be a means of putting together the various ideas and concepts of a wide variety of individuals in order to assemble a great range of knowledge and information. This proves to be invaluable to businesses and other organizations that require both general and specialist forms of knowledge from as many viable sources as possible.

Mass collaboration has become a reality as a result of fairly recent technological innovations. These include wireless Internet, high speed Internet, and various Internet based tools for collaboration, such as wikis, blogs, and others. Through these means, individuals from literally all over the planet can effectively share ideas and discourse back and forth via the Internet and even Internet based conferences, without being limited to certain geographical locations or challenges. Thanks to these forms of collaboration in both business and other forms, the possibilities of improving a project's results are practically endless.

Commercial Paper

Commercial paper proves to be a corporation-issued short term form of debt instrument which is unsecured. This paper is generally used to finance such things as inventories, accounts receivable, and other short term liabilities. The maturity dates for commercial paper vary, but they do not typically run any more than 270 days. Such paper instruments are generally issued at discounts to their face value. These discounts take into account the market interest rates that are effective when the company issues its paper.

Because commercial paper does not come with any underlying collateral, it turns out to be unsecured corporate debt. This means that only those companies that boast debt ratings which are highest quality will be able to find takers easily. Other companies must float their paper debt issues at greater discounts. This makes the funds come at a higher cost. Large organizations issue these paper instruments in significant denominations of typically $100,000 or higher. The most usual buyers of these paper instruments are banks and financial institutions, other companies, money market funds, and wealthy investors.

Commercial paper offers significant advantages for the corporations who utilize it. One of the biggest is that they do not have to register these offerings with the SEC Securities and Exchange Commission if the paper reaches maturity within 270 days or before nine months pass. This makes it a cost effective and quick way to obtain finance. While companies do have up to 270 days before the SEC is involved, typical maturity time frames for this paper only average around 30 days.

There are some restrictions to the use of commercial paper. It's funds can only be utilized for current assets and inventories. They may not be employed to purchase fixed assets like new facilities or plants unless the SEC is involved.

The financial crisis that began to erupt in 2007 involved the commercial paper market in a significant way. When investors had fears that major companies like Lehman brothers had problems with their liquidity and financial condition, markets for commercial paper seized up. Companies lost their access to funding which was affordable and simple to obtain.

This market freezing also led to money market funds "breaking the buck." As major investors in these paper instruments, the funds suffered from the suspect health of firms whose issued paper caused their own fund values to drop below the standard $1. Up to this point, money market funds had been considered risk free for investors. Government backing and guarantees were required to restore order and functionality to these markets.

A company might need additional short time frame funds in order to pay for Christmas holiday season additional inventory. The company could issue paper for $20 million in needs at $20.2 million face value. This means investors will provide it with $20 million in funding and receive $200,000 as interest when the paper matures. It would amount to a 1% interest rate. If the paper is not redeemed at its initial maturity, the interest rate would adjust the amount of principal and interest the paper would return appropriately based on the number of days it remained outstanding.

Conversion Discount

Conversion Discount refers to a special option applied to conversion investments. Understanding what a conversion is first becomes necessary in order to make sense of the discount clause. Conversions are the abilities to exchange some from of a convertible debt instrument into another kind of asset such as company stock. This conversion will be contractually spelled out at a prearranged price for a pre-set date deadline. The feature of a conversion itself proves to be a financial derivative type of instrument which has a separate and distinct value from the security itself. This is why including a conversion option in a security will only increase its all around value to the potential buyers.

Convertible bonds are excellent examples of assets that go through conversions and may end up with these discounts. Such a bond provides the holders with the ability to trade in the bond for a previously arranged quantity of stock in the company which issued the bond. This would usually be attractive to the holders of the bonds when the stock shares' value is greater than that of the bond itself. This is the point when most bond holders choose to exercise their conversion clause.

Looking at a tangible example helps to clarify the issue. Consider that Paul has a convertible bond from Astra Zeneca the Anglo-Swedish pharmaceutical company. The bond has a value of $1,000. Should Paul have the option to convert this bond into 10 shares of Astra Zeneca stock, then he will probably choose to do so only if the stock is worth more than $100 per share. This would give him equity holdings greater than the $1,000 original value of the company bond.

The idea becomes interesting with discounts. The interest rates on such bonds is often very low, even less than five to six percent. This does not fairly compensate investors for the risks they often take on with companies that have non-established track records, insecure income streams, or shaky credit. Because of this, investors can be additionally compensated with the option to convert the note into equity. Once upon a time in the early years of the 2000's, companies used to set this up as a stock warrant. In the last ten plus years they have been using conversion discounts with these notes instead.

Conversions discounts are quite attractive for investors. They do not simply deliver an options to buy a stock at a given time in the future as warrants do. Instead, they provide the right (but usually not the obligation) to convert into the stock at a lower price for every share (compared to other buyers) in a certain Qualified Financing event of the convertible notes. Naturally the investors' benefits in this are far more instantaneous than with warrants. They are not required to wait for a company sale in order to buy more shares. They also receive these shares instead of having to buy them all over again, as with warrants. This means that no exercise price applies. This conversion discounted price for shares actually pays the cost of the additional shares which they are provided in the round of Qualified Financing.

As a result, they are getting more shares for their money. This is because the conversion discount is commonly 20 percent to 40 percent or even higher. As a concrete example, if the holder of a conversion note in the Cancer Cure Company offers the conversion discount at 30 percent, then for every seventy cents of the note the bond holder owns, he will receive a dollar face value share of stock.

Convertible Bond

A convertible bond is like a hybrid between a stock and a bond. Corporations issue these bonds which the bondholders may choose to convert into shares of the underlying company stock whenever they decide. Such a bond usually pays better yields than do shares of common stocks. Their yields are also typically less than regular corporate bonds pay.

Convertible bonds provide income to their investors just as traditional corporate bonds do. These convertibles also possess the unique ability to gain in price if the stock of the issuing company does well. The reasoning behind this is straightforward. Because the bond has the ability to be directly converted into stock shares, the security's value will only gain as the stock shares themselves actually rise on the market.

When the stock performs poorly, the investors do not have the ability to convert the convertible bond into shares. They only gain the yield as a return on the investment in this case. The advantage these bonds have over the company stock in these deteriorating conditions is significant.

The value of the convertible instrument will only drop to its par value as long as the company that issues it does not go bankrupt. This is because on the specified maturity date, investors will obtain back their original principal. It is quite correct to say that these types of bonds typically have far less downside potential than do shares of common stocks.

There are disadvantages as well as advantages to these convertible bonds. Should the issuer of the bond file for bankruptcy, investors in these kinds of bonds possess a lower priority claim on the assets of the corporation than do those who invested in debt which was not convertible. Should the issuer default or not make an interest or principal payment according to schedule, the convertibles will likely suffer more than a regular corporate bond would. This is the flip side to the higher potential to appreciate which convertibles famously possess. It is a good reason that individuals who choose to invest in single convertible securities should engage in significant and extended research on the issuer's credit.

It is also important to note that the majority of these convertible bonds can be called. This gives the issuer the right to call away the bonds at a set share price. It limits the maximum gain an investor can realize even if the stock significantly outperforms. This means that a convertible security will rarely offer the identical unlimited gain possibilities which common stocks can.

If investors are determined to do the necessary research on an individual company, they can purchase a convertible bond from a broker. For better convertible diversification, there are numerous mutual funds which invest in only convertible securities. These funds are provided by a variety of major mutual fund companies.

Some of the biggest are Franklin Convertible Securities, Vanguard Convertible Securities, Fidelity Convertible Securities, and Calamos Convertible A. Several ETF exchange traded funds provide a similar convertible diversification with lower service charges. Among these are the SPDR Barclays Capital Convertible Bond ETF and the PowerShares Convertible Securities Portfolio.

It is important to know that the bigger convertible securities portfolios such as the ETFs track have a tendency to match the performance of the stock market quite closely in time. This makes them similar to a high dividend equity fund. Such investments do offer possible upside and diversification when measured against typical holdings of bonds. They do not really offer much in the way of diversification for individuals who already keep most of their investment dollars in stocks.

Corporate Bonds

Corporate bonds are debt securities that a company issues and sells to investors. Such corporate bonds are generally backed by the company's ability to repay the loan. This money is anticipated to result from successful operations in the future time periods. With some corporate bonds, the physical assets of a company can be offered as bond collateral to ease investors' minds and any concerns about repayment.

Corporate bonds are also known as debt financing. These bonds provide a significant capital source for a great number of businesses. Other sources of capital for the companies include lines of credit, bank loans, and equity issues like stock shares. For a business to be capable of achieving coupon rates that are favorable to them by issuing their debt to members of the public, a corporation will have to provide a series of consistent earnings reports and to show considerable earnings potential. As a general rule, the better a corporation's quality of credit is believed to be, the simpler it is for them to offer debt at lower rates and float greater amounts of such debt.

Such corporate bonds are always issued in $1,000 face value blocks. Practically all of them come with a standardized structure for coupon payments. Some corporate bonds include what is known as a call provision. These provisions permit the corporation that issues them to recall the bonds early if interest rates change significantly. Every call provision will be specific to the given bond.

These types of corporate bonds are deemed to be of greater risk than are government issued bonds. Because of this perceived additional risk, the interest rates almost always turn out to be higher with corporate bonds. This is true for companies whose credit is rated as among the best.

Regarding tax issues of corporate bonds, these are pretty straight forward. The majority of corporate bonds prove to be taxable, assuming that their terms are for longer than a single year. To avoid taxes until the end, some bonds come with zero coupons and redemption values that are high, meaning that taxes are deferred as capital gains until the end of the bond term. Such corporate debts that come due in under a year are generally referred to as commercial paper.

Corporate bonds are commonly listed on the major exchanges and ECN's like MarketAxess and Bonds.com. Even though these bonds are carried on the major exchanges, their trading does not mostly take place on them. Instead, the overwhelming majority of such bonds trading occurs in over the counter and dealer based markets.

Among the various types of corporate bonds are secured debt, unsecured debt, senior debt, and subordinated debt. Secured debts have assets underlying them. Senior debts provide the strongest claims on the corporation's assets if the venture defaults on its debt obligations. The higher up an investor's bond is in the firm's capital structure, the greater their claim will ultimately be in such an unfortunate scenario as default or bankruptcy.

Corporation

A corporation refers to a business entity where it is distinctive and separated from the owners. Such corporations may take on many responsibilities similar to individuals. They can borrow and loan out money, make and execute contracts, hire and terminate employees, sue or become sued, pay taxes, and own cash and assets. This is why corporations are many times referred to by the phrase of legal person.

A corporation is a legal construct that controls and runs businesses of all types all over the globe. There may be differing legal arrangements from one government jurisdiction to the next, but they all have the attribute of a limited liability. With this protection, shareholders enjoy important rights like benefitting from dividends as a result of profits and price appreciation from successful business endeavors. While enjoying these advantages, limited liability means that they do not carry any of the personal responsibility for payment of the company's debts.

Practically every famous business and brand in the world is a part of a corporation. This includes such internationally recognized entities as Coca-Cola, McDonalds, Microsoft, and Toyota Motors. Corporations can also do business under a different name. A classic example of this is Alphabet Inc. that runs Google.

Corporations are established as a group of stock holders choose to incorporate. They pursue this follow up after a common goal in their ownership of the business. Such corporations may be charitable as well as for profit. The overwhelming majority of such companies are founded with the ambition of earning positive returns for the stock holders. These shareholders own some percentage of the corporation in exchange for paying for their shares. If they obtain them directly from the company, then their payments remit to the treasury of the company itself.

Corporations sometimes possess thousands of shareholders, especially when they are publicly traded companies. These entities could also have only a few or even one shareholder. The most common corporations within the United States are called "C Corporations."

Shareholders use their one vote per share to vote for the company board of directors every year. This group is responsible for naming the management which they oversee. The managers run the daily activities of the company. It is the corporation's board of directors which must carry out the business plan of the entity. They also do not bear responsibility for the company's debts, but have a fiduciary responsibility to care for the corporation. If they do not fulfill the duty faithfully, they may become personally liable for mistakes. There are tax statutes that allow for board of directors members to be personally liable.

As these corporations fulfill their goals, they can be wound down through a process also known as liquidation. In this process, they appoint a liquidator to sell off the company assets, pay the creditors, and share out all cash assets which remain among the stockholders. This can be done as a result of an involuntary or a voluntary procedure. Creditors can force liquidation when a company can no longer pay its debts. This often leads to corporate bankruptcy.

Cost of Goods Sold (COGS)

The Cost of Goods Sold refers to those costs which directly arise from the creation of a firm's goods or services. The phrase also sometimes is summarized by its acronym COGS or by an alternative name the "cost of sales." It will cover many expenses. Among these are all of the materials the company utilizes to physically produce the goods.

It also considers the labor expenses employed to create the items. It will not include expenses that are considered to be indirect. This means that sales force and distribution expenses will not be taken into account. COGS shows up on income statements. Accountants and economists can utilize it to subtract it out from the given company's revenues in order to establish the firm's gross margin.

Every business has the ultimate goal to earn profits at the heart of what it is doing. This is why a less expensive goods production for their product or service will lead to higher profits, all else being equal. A fuller explanation of what the Cost of Goods Sold includes involves inventory, materials, labor, factory equipment for production, and even overhead. All of these factors of production directly pertain to the goods or services the company produces. The calculation also takes into consideration the freight or shipping of inputs utilized. It would never include associated costs like rent for a facility or general payrolls of a company.

Looking at an example helps to clarify the Cost of Goods Sold concept. Where an automobile manufacturer is concerned, there will be a number of material costs. Chief among these would be those parts that actually combine to produce the car, as well as the cost of labor for assembling the car. The COGS would not include the cost of the sales force personnel which actually sell the car nor the price for getting the cars out to the dealership. Both of these last ideas are post-production costs, so they are not a part of the primary COGS.

There are a number of different ways for calculating the Cost of Goods Sold. It also varies from one certain kind of business to those in another industry. Among the most simple means of figuring this number out is to start with the costs of inventory over the production period. Next they would add in the aggregate purchase amounts in the same time frame. They would likely then subtract out the inventory at the end of production point. Such a calculation will provide the literal cost of the inventory which the company produced in a given time frame.

Another example helps to make the explanation clearer. Assume that a firm begins its production phase with $15 million worth of inventory. If they make $3 million in additional purchase in this time and end the production period with $14 million of inventory, then the firm's Cost of Goods Sold is calculated by taking the $15 million and adding in the $3 million in purchases and subtracting out the final $14 million in remaining inventory. This gives a final COGS of $15M plus $3M minus $14M for a final result of $4M.

The significance to this formula and Cost of Goods Sold figure is important. The COGS reveals how effectively the firm is able to convert its inventory into revenues and profits. This is why it is critical to compare the COGS against the revenue of the period under consideration. When the company above had a revenue exceeding $4 million, then it would boast a gross profit that was positive. If the revenue of the firm in question was less than the $4 million COGS, then there would be a negative gross profit. In other words, understanding and knowing the COGS figure for a company tells investors which companies are ultimately successful and which are in financial trouble, assuming that state of (negative profit) affairs continues for long.

Credit Analysis

Credit analysis refers to a kind of detailed consideration of a corporation or similar agency which issues debt. It is performed by managers of bond portfolios and investors. They seek to determine the ability of the borrower to cover their obligations of debt with this type of analysis. The ultimate goal is to discern the correct amount of default risk which investing in that specific agency or company will entail.

There are a number of different considerations in performing this credit analysis. Some of these are fixed expenses, operating margins, cash flows, and overhead costs. These are also considered in equity analysis, yet with a different emphasis. It is true that stronger credit ratings do not equate to any guarantee of impressive share price performance. Yet when investors grasp a company's credit ratings and the implications, they are able to better assess both the debt and equity results for a given corporation.

Financial elements of a particular company are extremely important in credit analysis. Analysts will consider incoming revenues as well as costs and expenses of the corporation. These will be assessed both as stand-alone values and versus the competitors in the industry. For a firm to be considered strong where credit is concerned, its overhead must permit it to attain better than average profit levels in all points of the business life cycle. Even in a downturn in the economy, stronger companies can deliver results which are higher than average for the industry. Stronger firms also can demonstrate pricing power. This represents the capability of passing on cost increases for inputs and raw materials to the customers via higher prices.

Competitive position is also important in a thorough credit analysis. Only companies which are strong competitively will be capable of maintaining their financial performances in the future. Companies which are highly competitive show long-running positive trends and abilities with quality of service, development of new products, and customer retention and satisfaction levels. It also helps a company's competitive position when there are effective barriers to competition. These can be in the form of protective regulations, substantial copyright and/or patent protections, or agreements on licensing, permits, and franchising.

The business environment is a third area of consideration for those performing credit analyses. This refers to three primary areas known as country risk, currency risk, and industry risk. Country risk relates to the ways in which the business activities of the enterprise can be negatively impacted by changes in the tax, regulatory, social, legal, and political regimes in those nations where they have a significant business presence.

Currency risk simply refers to the effects of drastic foreign exchange movements on both the corporate balance sheet and the company's capabilities of sourcing raw materials and other inputs or of selling their goods and products abroad. Industry risk pertains to the dynamics of the business, regulatory regime, and legal and market elements within the industry. These considerations can impact not only the industry but a particular company being evaluated by credit analysis.

Looking at some examples of this can help to better understand the concept. Where there are currency exposures throughout the supply chain, the company could hedge these appropriately in the futures markets. Another example is that the company may know its earnings will not change much even as their industry segment progresses along a change in technology.

There are many parallels between credit ratings of even different borrowing entities. This is why though the risk profile on an AAA-rated state government is less than that of an AAA-rated corporation, triple A rated borrowers in either scenario will always be far safer and less risky than the comparable B- and especially C-rated borrowers in each field. As an example, the A-rated S&P 500 companies boasted an average return of 10.74% in the period ending August 30th of 2013. For those same S&P companies with BB or lower credit ratings, their average return over the identical time period proved to be only 6.53%.

Credit Derivatives

Credit derivatives refer to bilateral contracts which are privately held. These contracts permit the holders to manage their credit risk exposure. Such derivatives turn out to be financial assets. Examples of the better-known ones in the derivatives universe are swaps, forward contracts, and options. The price of these is necessarily based upon the credit risk of economic entities like governments, companies, or private investors. This means that banks which are worried about one of their customers not being capable of repaying their loan are able to purchase protection against such a potential loss in default. They do this by keeping the loan on their books at the same time as they transfer the credit risk off to a third party more commonly referred to as the "counter party."

Such credit derivatives are only one of numerous different kinds of financial instruments available to investors and financial institutions today. With these derivatives, they are merely instruments whose existence derives from underlying financial instruments. The value which underlies them comes from a stock or other asset.

Two different principal forms of derivatives exist. These are calls and puts. Calls provide the right but not obligation to purchase a stock for a pre-set price called the strike price. Puts deliver the right but not obligation to sell particular stocks for pre-arranged strike prices. With either calls or puts, investors are obtaining insurance in case a stock price rises or falls. This makes every form of derivative product an insurance vehicle and particularly these credit derivative examples.

Numerous credit derivatives exist on the markets today. Among these are CDO Collateralized Debt Obligations, CDS Credit Default Swamps, credit default swap options, total return swaps, and credit spread forwards. Banks are allowed to utilize these complicated instruments in order to completely take away their default risk from even an entire loan portfolio. The financial institutions or banks pay a premium, or upfront fee, for this accommodation.

Considering a concrete example helps to make the credit derivatives concept clearer. Plants R Us borrows $200,000 off of a bank with a ten year repayment term. Because Plants R Us shows a poor credit history, they are forced to buy the bank a credit derivative in order to be able to receive the loan. The bank accepts this product which will permit them to transfer all of the default risk to a third counter party. This means that the counter party would be forced to deliver all unpaid interest and principal on the loan in the event that Plants R Us defaults on the said loan. For this guarantee, Plants R Us pays an annual fee to the counter party for their assumed risk. Should the Plants R Us not default on the loan, then the counterparty firm keeps the entire fee. This makes it a win-win-win situation for all three parties. The bank is protected against a default by Plants R Us, which gets to have its loan. The counter party collects the yearly fee. All parties gain and benefit from the arrangement.

Credit derivatives' values vary widely depending on several factors. These include the borrower's credit quality as well as the counter party's credit quality. The biggest concern comes down to the credit quality of the third party - counter party. If the counter party defaults or is otherwise unable to honor their commitments specified in the derivatives contract, then the financial institution will not get its payment for the loan principal and interest. The counter party would naturally no longer receive its annual premium payments any longer either. This is why the quality of credit for the counter party is so much more critical than is the credit quality of the borrower (Plants R Us in the example).

Credit History

Credit history is an official record that shows the company or personal history of borrowing and paying back loans. This history provides business or personal identifying information, a record of credit that the individual or company has, and negative elements such as bankruptcies and late payments.

It describes how individuals use their money and finances. It lists out the number of credit cards, loans and other obligations, and bills that a consumer has. It keeps records of whether they pay these bills in a timely fashion. The credit history information is compiled as companies send in data on credit cards and loans to one of the three main credit bureaus. These are Experian, Equifax, and TransUnion. They act as the gatekeepers of credit history.

These companies compile all of this information on credit and bills into a file called a credit report. This credit report is the repository of all an individual's credit history. It contains a great deal of personal information that starts with the owner's name, social security number, and address. All credit cards and loans are itemized out and detailed. It states the total money a person owes. Finally, credit reports put together a profile on the individuals as to whether they pay their bills late or on time.

Credit history and credit reports are important for individuals. Businesses will not loan out money to people until they know all about them and their spending and borrowing habits and past. Businesses find all of this information on personal credit history in these credit reports and then make decisions as to whether they will extend credit in the form of a credit card or make a loan to the applicant.

Some employers choose to examine a candidate's credit report along with a job application. Insurance companies also consider it when they are determining rates of their customers. Even cell phone and utility companies often look it up when they are deciding how much a person will need to pay in deposits to start service.

Credit history is also used to create a credit score. Credit scores are numbers that the three credit reporting bureaus maintain for individuals using their credit history. If the credit history is good, then the credit score will be as well. Individuals can see their credit history and obtain their credit reports for free every year. Credit scores are not available unless people pay for them.

High credit scores convey a good credit history. Lower credit scores refer to a poor credit history for an individual. Each of the three credit bureau companies will have a slightly different score for a person. High credit scores range from 700-850. Low credit scores start from 300 to 600.

Credit history as shown in a personal credit report is very important to know. Each of the three companies is required to send individuals their credit report every year showing personal credit history on demand. Individuals are able to request this at no charge by going to AnnualCreditReport.com.

There are other companies that advertise offers to provide credit scores for free along with free credit reports. These are usually promotional offers that require individuals to sign up for a monthly service of some type in order to qualify for them. Such offers are often monthly credit monitoring services for a fee. As a rule, a person will generally have to pay something to obtain his or her credit scores.

Credit Ratings Agencies

Credit Ratings Agencies are those companies whose purpose is to consider and report on the financial strength which firms and government agencies demonstrate. They report on national as well as international corporations and agencies in this capacity. Their reports are most interested in the ability of the entities in question to fulfill their obligations for both principal and interest repayments of their bonds and other kinds of debts. Besides this, the various ratings agencies carefully examine and review the conditions and terms on every debt issue.

The end result of the agencies' work is to release a credit rating on both the debt issues in particular and the debt issuers more generally. When they agencies have high confidence that the issuer will be able to meet their debt servicing of principal and interest as promised, they will issue a high credit rating. When the opposite is true, the credit rating will be lower. It is entirely possible for a particular issue of debt to receive a differing credit rating from the issuer. This heavily depends on the particular terms of the issuer.

The impacts of these debt issue ratings are enormous in the industry and for the specific issuers in question. Those debt issues that obtain the best credit ratings will receive the most attractive interest rates from the credit markets. This is because the confidence of investors in an entity's capability of making their various payment obligations comes down to the credit ratings agencies review, analyses and especially ratings. Since the interest rates which investors demand for a specific debt issue will be inversely correlated to the borrower's particular creditworthiness, weaker borrowers will have to pay more while the stronger ones will enjoy paying less.

In this way, the credit ratings agencies act on behalf of businesses in much the same capacity as the consumer credit bureaus do for individual consumers. Such credit scores which the credit bureaus develop for individual people will greatly impact the interest rates at which individuals are able to borrow money.

The downside to these credit ratings agencies and their work is that they have been made the scapegoat for company and government defaults in recent years. Their research quality in particular has been the target of heavy criticism from observers and analysts who point out companies which they rated highly suddenly collapsed. Governments in Europe on which they provided high credit ratings defaulted or almost defaulted on their debts, as with Greece in particular.

This caused third party observers to argue that the various credit ratings agencies are actually poor at financial forecasting, at uncovering growing and negative trends for the debt issuers they follow, and also are overly late in revising down their ratings. Besides this, critics point to the many conflicts of interest of the ratings agencies. This is because the debt issuers are able to pick out and pay the ratings agencies for the reviews of their bonds. In a survey conducted in 2008, 11 percent of the various investment professionals surveyed by the CFA Institute responded that they had observed personally instances where the major ratings agencies had actually upgraded their given ratings on bonds when they were pressured by the debt issuers in question.

There are only three firms today which dominate the space, and this is part of the problem. The Wall Street Journal provided the ratings shares of the big 3 agencies in their 2011 report. Of the 2.8 million ratings they issue collectively (with the other seven minor agencies), S&P 500 controls the greatest market share with 42.2 percent. Moody's holds 36.9 percent of the market. Fitch rounds out the top three with 17.9 percent.

The article claimed that fully 95 percent of all revenues in this industry were earned by the big three. Only 2.9 percent of the ratings issued came from the other seven firms. The other seven credit ratings agencies were A.M. Best, DBRS, Japan Credit Rating Agency, Rating and Investment Info., Egan-Jones Ratings, Morningstar Credit Ratings, and Kroll Bond Rating Agency.

Between the top two issuers Moody's and Standard & Poor's, they provide ratings for roughly 80 percent of all municipal and corporate bond issues. They are typically regarded as a level higher than Fitch. One particular example speaks volumes. While Egan-Jones had downgraded the U.S. Federal government debt to the second highest rating years earlier, it was ignored largely by the markets and world. When Standard & Poor's took the same action by downgrading the Federal government of the United

States debt to AA+ on August 5th of 2011, this shook the world bond, currency, and stock markets. It demonstrates the clout S&P and Moody's especially enjoy over all of their various credit ratings agencies rivals.

Credit Risk

Credit Risk pertains to the possibilities that borrowers might not be able to pay back their loan. This means that the lender would potentially lose its loan principal amount as well as the interest which goes along with it. Such risk occurs as a result of a borrower premise.

The borrowers almost always believe that they will be able to utilize their cash flows from the future in order to pay back their currently agreed upon debts. The reality is that it is practically impossible to guarantee that borrowers will certainly receive those ongoing funds in order to pay back their debts. The reward that issuers receive for taking on such credit risk is the interest payments which borrowers deliver to the issuers of the debt.

Lenders provide credit cards, mortgages, auto loans, and even personal loans to consumers and businesses. Regardless of how strong a candidate may appear on paper, there is always some chance and risk that the borrower will in fact default on the loan obligation. This is much like when a business provides credit to one of its clients. The chances exist that the client may be incapable of paying their invoices to the company.

The phrase credit risk similarly refers to the danger that bond issuers may be unable to deliver their scheduled payments. It could also mean that an insurance company cannot honor a claim on a purchased policy.

The credit risks are figured using the borrower's total capability of repaying a debt. Assessing credit risks on loans made to consumers involves reviewing and considering what analysts call the "Five C's." These are the consumers' capacity to pay back, their credit history, their collateral, their capital, and their conditions of the loan.

Investors who are contemplating purchasing or investing in a bond also must consider the bond and firm's underlying credit rating. With a lower rating, the government entity or corporation is in danger of defaulting. It means they have a high risk for default. Alternatively, when such organizations enjoy higher ratings, analysts will call them safer investments.

It is up to the likes of credit risk agencies including Moody's and Fitch to evaluate the various risks posed by literally thousands of municipalities and corporate bond issuers. They do this continuously in what amounts to an enormous undertaking.

Investors which want to take on a limited amount of credit risk will choose to purchase bonds from municipalities with AAA (triple A) rated credit. When they do not care about some risk in the investment, they could instead pick out a bond that boasts a lesser rating. In compensation for this risk, they will receive potentially more interest in the form of a higher interest rate.

Sometimes there will be a greater perceived risk of default from a bond issuer or borrower. In these cases, investors or lenders would insist on a greater interest rate return for the danger in which they are placing their capital. Examples of this abound. Mortgage applicants who possess fantastic credit ratings as well as a consistent income from a historically stable job will be considered a lower credit risk. This means they will enjoy a better interest rate for their mortgage.

Alternatively, those applicants with poor credit history and scores from the three main credit bureaus will be forced into dealing with a subprime lender. These often predatory types of lenders provide loans with quite high interest rates to those borrowers considered to be higher risk individuals.

The same is true with bond issuers. Those that have ratings which are less perfect will be forced to offer greater interest rates and amounts to investors. The bond issuers in the opposite camp with unblemished credit ratings will enjoy lower rates on their proffered bonds. This is simply because those bond issuers with poorer credit quality will have to engage in offers of higher returns. This is so they can attract investors who would then be taking on a substantial risk of the bonds not being repaid in a timely fashion.

Credit Suisse

Credit Suisse is a leading global Swiss-based banking giant whose history stretches back to 1856. Their global reach is supported by operations in more than 50 different countries. This banking group maintains over 48,000 employees who hail from more than 150 different countries around the globe. Their broad international reach allows the bank to create a well-balanced revenue stream geographically and helps them to engage in significant opportunities for growth throughout the globe.

Credit Suisse serves its international clientele in three divisions which are regionally focused. These are the Swiss Universal Bank, the International Wealth Management, and the Asia Pacific divisions. The three principle divisions receive support from Global Markets and Investment Banking & Capital Markets support divisions.

The Swiss Universal Bank focuses on the home country market of Switzerland. Here Credit Suisse delivers a significant variety of financial products and services to corporate, private, and institutional clients residing generally in Switzerland. The Private Banking business here is one of the leading brands in the country.

More than 1.6 million individuals or entities count themselves as customers of this business of the bank. This includes not only regular retail clients, but also affluent and ultra high net worth individuals (HNWI). Included in this division is their Bank-now consumer finance business. This division also provides top of the line service, technology, and platform support for asset managers throughout Switzerland. The bank within Switzerland is comprised of 184 branches and 1,570 relationship managers. Included in this is their affiliate bank Neue Aargauer Bank.

The Swiss Universal Bank division also has the Corporate and Institutional Banking business. It provides best in class services and advice to over 100,000 corporations, businesses, financial institutions, and commodity traders. Included in this business is their Swiss investment banking business. This division comprises 48 different locations and 490 relationship managers.

The second Credit Suisse division is the bank's International Wealth

Management. Here they take care of international institutional, corporate, and private clients by offering them expert advice and a wide variety of financial products and services. The Private Banking business helps wealthy individual clients and outside asset managers throughout Europe, Africa, the Middle East, and Latin America.

The bank maintains 46 locations and 1,200 relationship managers. Besides their own products, they also represent a number of third party services and products. The Asset Management business provides investment products and services worldwide to governments, pension funds, endowments, foundations, individuals, and corporations. This business concentrates on both traditional as well as alternative asset allocations and strategies.

The third Credit Suisse division is the group's Asia Pacific group. Here they focus on providing financial services and products to their high net worth and ultra high net worth individual clients, as well as corporate, entrepreneur, and institutional customers. The group offers its clients integrated access and support to the wider financial markets, specific financing solutions, and numerous products.

Within this division, the Private Banking business offers tailored products and services that include digital access to the private banking services. They maintain 13 locations throughout 7 countries and 590 relationship managers within them. The Investment Banking business in this division advises their important clients on merger and acquisition deals, on takeover defense strategies and divestitures. Also on corporate restructuring and sales, and offers debt and equity underwriting services to institutions and individual and business clients.

Besides this, the Investment Banking business covers trading and sales of both equities and fixed income instruments and offers a variety of derivatives, equity and debt securities, and opportunities for financing for its sovereign, corporate, and institutional customers.

Credit Suisse's core strengths remain its leading worldwide reputation and presence as a wealth manger, its impressive market share in home country Switzerland, and its particular skills and abilities in investment banking.

Debt Coverage Ratio (DCR)

Debt coverage ratio has different meanings dependent on what entity is using it. In the world of corporate finance, it is the amount of cash flow that a company has to service its current debts. This ratio utilizes the net operating income divided by the debt payments due in a year or less. This includes principal, interest, lease payments, and the sinking fund.

It has a different meaning with governments and individuals. For finances of a national government, debt coverage ratio refers to the export earnings required for the country to make its yearly principal and interest payments with the external debts of the nation. With individual finance, banks and their loan officers utilize this ratio to decide on income property loans.

Debt coverage ratios must be higher than one in order for the government, company, or individual to prove enough income to satisfy its present debt obligations. With a DCR under 1, it lacks the means to do so. This ratio is determined by dividing Net Operating Income by the Total Debt Service.

The net operating income turns out to be the revenue of a company less its operating expenses. This does not cover interest payments or taxes. The NOI can also equate to the EBIT Earnings Before Interest and Tax. Investors and lenders which are evaluating the creditworthiness of corporations and companies should use criteria that is consistent when they figure out the DCR.

Total debt service is the term that concerns the present debt obligations. This will include principal, interest, lease payments, and sinking fund all owed in the next year. Balance sheets also include both the long term debt current portion and the short term debt.

When a debt coverage ratio is lower than one, it says that the entity cash flow is negative. With a DCR of .90, the company would only possess sufficient NOI to handle 90% of their yearly debt payments. With personal finance this would mean that the borrower had to access some outside funds each month in order to cover the payments. Lenders usually discourage loans with negative cash flow. They may permit them when the borrower can show a strong outside income.

Lenders almost always consider the debt coverage ratio of borrowers before they extend loans to them. They do not want to loan money to entities with lower than one. Such groups will have to draw on sources outside of their traditional income or borrow more in order to make their debt payments. When the DCR is dangerously close to one, then the borrower is considered to be vulnerable to a slowdown in income. Only a minor setback to its cash flow would mean it would not be able to service the debts. Some lenders will actually insist that the borrowers keep minimum levels of debt coverage ratios while they have a loan balance. In these cases, borrowers whose ratios decline below this minimum level are in technical default.

Lenders can be more lenient on debt coverage ratios when the economy is booming. An expanding economy means that credit is available more easily. This often causes lenders to work with companies and individuals on their lower ratios. The problem is that borrowers which are under qualified can impact the stability of the economy.

In the 2008 financial crisis, subprime borrowers received credit in the form of mortgages without proper consideration of their finances. As such borrowers defaulted in large numbers, the lenders that had made loans to them failed. The largest savings and loan institution Washington Mutual turned out to be the most egregious example of this scenario.

Debt Restructuring

Debt restructuring refers to a means which corporations or countries with overwhelming debt loads utilize to change the terms of their outstanding debt arrangements so they can gain advantage in repayment. Corporations will often utilize a form of debt restructuring so that they can sidestep defaulting on their already existing debt levels. They might also wish to gain the benefits of lower interest rates that may be available to them on the markets.

One way that companies accomplish this is by issuing a series of callable bonds. These permit them to easily and rapidly restructure their new debts at a given point in the future. In this case, the firms' existing debts will be called. They will then replace them with a newer issued debt for the lower, more advantageous interest rate. Another way that corporations are able to restructure their debt lies in changing the provisions and terms of the current debt issue.

With corporate debt restructuring, a company will typically reorganize its actual obligations by lowering the debt burdens on their firm. They can do this by reducing the payable rates on the debt or by extending the amount of time they have until they repay the debt obligations. By doing either of these, the company ensures it is able to service its relevant debt burdens. There are other cases where the creditors will opt to forgive a part of the debt in exchange for obtaining an equity stake in the firm.

A need for this type of corporate debt restructuring most often occurs when corporations or companies are experiencing financial difficulties. These make it most difficult to keep up with their full range of financial obligations. Sometimes such troubles can be sufficient to create a significant risk of the company declaring bankruptcy. In these cases, they have the ability to engage in a structured negotiation with the creditors to lower the burdens so that they can avoid entering bankruptcy-led defaults.

Within the United States, there is a provision of the corporate bankruptcy code known as Chapter 11. These protocols permit corporations to obtain effective protection from their creditors so that they are able to try to rearrange the debt terms to continue on as a reorganized, ongoing, viable concern. Thanks to federal bankruptcy courts becoming involved in this process, even when the creditors refuse to accept such a settlement and reorganization, the courts can mandate that the creditors accept the plan if they deem it to be reasonable and fair.

It is not only corporations and companies which can avail themselves of such debt restructuring. Governments also have needs for help with their debts when they finally become unsustainable. This is not a new phenomenon. It stretches back to the first historically recorded sovereign debt default of the fourth century B.C. At this time, ten different Greek city-states defaulted on loans they had taken from the sacred temple of Delos. Despite the fact that this has occurred for at least 2,300 years, today no clear and mutually understood rules exist to structure the process for what will occur if a sovereign state can not pay their debts.

The most recent classic example of this dates back to the huge default by Argentina. Their enormous debt default in 2001 was among the largest in modern history. The rules are unclear as to who has jurisdiction and who can set restructuring terms. For years Argentina refused to negotiate terms with the eight percent of its bondholders who would not agree to the terms the country set in 2001. Then a court ruling from the U.S. Supreme Court confused the issue by ordering Argentina to settle with the remaining holdouts at full value plus interest before they could pay the agreed-upon settled amount to the other 92 percent of debt holders.

Argentina then came back to the table for the eight percent of mostly opportunistic hedge funds which had bought their defaulted debt for pennies on the dollar. Grudgingly under duress they paid the hedge fund eight percent claimants. This was an unusual case study that only worked out because the debt had been issued under American debt law. In other cases and scenarios, it is only the IMF International Monetary Fund that is attempting to create some sort of rules on situations like these.

Yet in the end, no one can force a country to pay its debts back to creditors short of going to war with them to seize their physical assets or by freezing assets of the offending country in the banks or vaults of the debt holders' countries.

Deferred Maintenance

Deferred maintenance proves to be the action of putting off maintenance procedures that are needed and routine on both personal property, such as machinery, or real estate property, such as infrastructure. This is done to save on expenses, to reassign money that is available in the budget, or to achieve the available levels of budget funding.

The downside to this avoidance or delay of generally needed repairs is that it causes the deterioration of assets, and finally their total impairment, if continued for an extended period of time. Usually over time, the practice of constantly deferring your maintenance will end up with greater costs in the future, the eventual failure of assets, and from time to time with safety and health concerns resulting.

Maintenance is one of the budgetary items that is forced to battle along side other needs' and programs' funding. Since the money is simply not always available for the category of maintenance's use, it is often short changed. Other times, the money is available until it is directed by management to higher priority assignments and requirements later.

Maintenance that is deferred is most usually not reported to the necessary parties right away. Many times, it is never even reported at all. Such deferred maintenance that goes on over a lack of funds appropriated to the cause will finally lead to a greater number of incidences of inefficient service for the public, possible safety dangers, operations that are inefficient and ineffective, and greater costs overall at a future point in time.

Examples of personal deferred maintenance and business deferred maintenance cases abound. Deferred maintenance in a home would include delaying the car's recommended one year inspection or tune up, or not having those repairs done that the mechanic recommended. As a result of this, the car will likely not operate as effectively or efficiently. It could also suffer mechanical or electrical failures or even become involved in an unnecessary crash over safety issues.

This term of deferred maintenance is more commonly used with large corporations or governments though. A large corporation slashing its budget might result in the company's plants and equipment not undergoing their annual cleaning and refurbishing.

The firm might get away with this for a year or even two. In time though, problems will begin to show up in machinery break down, equipment misses and failure, and possible shut downs of the plant, if this practice of ignoring critical plant maintenance is put off much or for too long.

Deficit Spending

Deficit spending is a generally unsustainable scenario where a greater number of resources are employed to secure purchases than are brought in to the organization through revenue generating means. When this is the case, the business or government outfit actually operates in a budget deficit.

This simply means that not enough financial resources are being created by the organization in order to effectively fund the operating budget. As this occurs, the additional expenses are paid for by utilizing deferred payment plans that permit the organization to buy now and pay later, or alternatively with credit accounts.

Even though such deficit spending can occur with consumers and businesses, it is generally discussed pertaining to governments and their operations. These days, governments are mostly incapable of running their operations without resorting to deficit spending. As the taxes that are collected generally are insufficient to cover all of the costs that are proposed by the annual budget, the shortfall is commonly covered by buying things with money that has been borrowed. In such a way, these governments run their activities in a deficit spending scenario.

Not every government runs its affairs from a negative budget scenario all of the time. There are periods where governments can look forward to the revenues that come in from taxes and any investments surpassing the money that is required to cover the costs of budgetary items. In these moments, governments have the opposite of deficit spending situations. They are running on budget surpluses. Surpluses are used for a variety of different needs, such as infrastructure improvements, repayment of debt from past deficit spending, or savings for future budget deficits.

Without a doubt, deficit spending proves to be all too common for governments. This does not make it a wise economic policy to pursue continuously over extended time frames. The reason for this is that deficit spending commonly requires borrowing funds that must be paid back with interest that accrues over time. In such a way, enormous amounts of government debt can be built up in short time frames.

Because of this, a number of responsible governments attempt to intelligently manage their deficit spending in such a way that they only engage in it to keep up critical operations and services that the citizens need for their well being. Other less important programs they try to cut back on whenever possible.

Companies may sometimes operate on a deficit spending basis. If they do this for long periods of time, then they are often unable to turn the failing trend around. The end result of this behavior leads to bankruptcy or being purchased by other, more fiscally responsible businesses. Consumers that engage in deficit spending for longer periods than only temporary time frames similarly discover that the scenario ends up in financial destruction. Outstanding assets may then be liquidated to satisfy the debts that result.

Demutualization

Demutualization is the decision undertaken by the members of a mutual corporation to convert their company into one which shareholders own instead. This means that the members and users of the mutual company give up their rights of use in exchange for stock shares in the new usually publically traded company.

Such mutual companies were originally established in order to offer specific services to their members. They are able to provide said services for the least expensive price possible to their members. This is because they are not forced to earn profits, as with publically traded or for profit corporations. Instead, their goals are to remain at least financially stable and solvent, to offer member benefits, and to return any profits that remain after they pay expenses to their member owners.

This has been a practice most common with insurance companies in recent years. A number of mutual insurers that could not earn sufficient returns on their investments, or which faced limited possibilities in acquisitions and mergers on their own, chose this path. They evolved into companies which were publically traded stock corporations. It has aided insurance companies in raising much-needed fresh capital. It also helped them to become more competitive in the domestic marketplace.

The question remains is this a good strategy for the mutual insurance company owners? They already enjoy the rights to elect the members of the board of directors. They also have some voice in the way the firms operate. All premiums which the owners pay go towards the insurance company's bottom line. If there is a profit, then a portion of those premiums are returned as dividends. This is not the case for those life insurance policy holders who own term life insurance only.

The insurance companies pay out these dividends once they determine what money remains after key expenses. Among these costs they look at are policy expenses, mortality payouts, and administration costs. Interestingly enough, mutual companies do not have to disclose to their owners how they come up with their dividends.

There are several important reasons why firms elect to pursue a demutualization. They are usually first and foremost interested in gaining greater access to additional capital. With this fresh infusion of substantial amounts of cash they can raise by selling shares, they are able to pursue mergers and acquisitions. The mutual insurance companies have found that laws which permit the mega banks and publically traded insurance companies to offer similar services have created huge amounts of pressure to compete effectively in the marketplace for financial services. At least on paper and on balance sheets, additional money a company obtains from its IPO initial public offering provides them with a healthier and more powerful firm.

The process of demutualization can require in the range of 18 to 24 months. Before the insurer can affect conversion, they will invest significant amounts of time to fashion a draft proposal. This has to first be approved by the board of directors of the firm. Next this proposal has to be turned in to the state's insurance department for review. The firm will also want to run meetings giving out information in the state where their head office is based. Policy holders must be informed with regards to their rights to vote yes or no on the final proposal.

Those policy holders which have a right to participate in the process are usually allowed to choose one of three benefits. They can request shares of stock in the publically traded company, a cash payout, or an enhancement to their existing policy. Finally, after the policy holders approve the demutualization process, it is up to the department insurance of the state to review the plan. They must give final approval to the decision for demutualization to commence.

Deutsche Bank

Deutsche Bank is the leading German bank in the world. It commands a substantial market share in Germany, a strong place in European banking, and an important presence in both the Asia Pacific and Americas regions.

The group has grown from its founding in Berlin, Germany in 1870 to encompass strong operating bases in all of the major developed and emerging markets. This gives them a solid prospect for business expansion in the world's rapidly growing markets, comprising Lain America, Central and Eastern Europe, and the Asia Pacific regions. Their important position in Europe provides the bank with a solid foundation from which to benefit not only from the resilient economic conditions in native market Germany, but also from rebounding strong corporate activity levels throughout the euro zone.

From Deutsche Bank's first international foray into Asia in 1872 on, the bank has always looked abroad for opportunities to expand. This has carried it into more than 70 nations around the world today. Of its 2,790 total branches, 1,827 are located in Germany and another 963 are found in other countries and markets beyond the bank's home base. With the ongoing theme of continuous globalization in the international economy dominating, this puts the banking group in a strong position. It has more than adequate diversification throughout different regions of the world and significant revenue streams coming in from all the major areas around the globe.

Deutsche Bank offers practical banking solutions and services to private individuals, medium and small businesses, corporations, institutional investors, and governments. They operate a number of businesses specifically focused on the needs of these client bases.

The Corporate Finance Business group takes responsibility for M&A merger and acquisition activities. This includes equity and debt issues, advisory services, and coverage of capital markets for medium to large corporations. They deliver this complete range of financial services and products to the business clients via industry- and regional- specific teams. A subdivision of this is the CIB Corporate & Investment Banking business. It combines the expertise of Deutsche Bank's corporate finance, commercial banking, and transaction banking under the direction of a single unified leadership team. It is made up of both the Corporate Finance and Global Transaction Banking businesses.

The Deutsche Bank Private & Business Clients Corporate business offers in branch financial and banking services to self employed entrepreneurs, private clients, and medium to small businesses on an international scale.

The bank's Wealth Management business provides high quality and extremely personalized services to the ultra high and high net worth families and individuals along with certain institutions. These particular clients receive a complete package of wealth management services, philanthropic activity advisory services, and inheritance planning advice.

The Asset Management business at Deutsche Bank delivers investment and mutual fund services and products to its retail clients around the world. The bank brands this franchise as the DWS Investments group. It also provides institutional clients of the bank like insurance companies and pension funds with a wide variety of services and products that range from traditional to alternative investments. Among these products and services are the DWS Funds, Deutsch Insurance Asset Management, DB Advisors Institutional Asset Management, and RREEF Real Estate Investment Management.

Deutsche Bank also operates a large and important Asia Pacific division of the bank. The company's history in Asia traces back to the first branches they opened in Shanghai, China and Yokohama, Japan which it founded in 1872. Nowadays the operation is quite a bit larger. The group maintains office presences in 16 national markets and employs 16,000 staff in Asia Pacific. The bank's Asia Pacific division headquarters are located in Singapore.

Discretionary Expenses

A discretionary expense refers to those business or home costs that are not considered to be critical for the entity to function or operate effectively. This is important, since both businesses and individuals often are required to pay for discretionary expenses using discretionary income.

As an example, businesses might permit their staff to charge specific kinds of entertainment and meal expenses to the firm when they engage in these activities to build up business ties with clients, vendors, or potential customers. They might also cover meals and entertainment simply to foster better relations with their staff. A home would refer to discretionary expenses as those that they do not need, but instead want to have.

Discretionary income refers to any funds which remain after businesses or individuals pay their taxes and mandatory costs. On an individual level, those persons who do not have any money left once they pay the bills do not have any discretionary income. In order for them to pay for a discretionary expenses, they will be forced to take on debt by obtaining a loan or utilizing credit cards. An example of using debt to pay for a discretionary expense is utilizing credit cards to pay for a family vacation.

There are two kinds of expenses which consumer households incur. Some they are required to pay according to the law. This includes income and other taxes as well as health insurance (at least in tax years 2014 and 2015). Costs they have to pay out in order to make sure the family and household functions are also non-discretionary in nature. These include transportation costs, food, utilities, and rent or mortgage.

The people making the money do not have a choice of whether or not to pay these costs every month without suffering sometimes-severe consequences. The other kind of cost qualifies as a discretionary expense. This would be luxury items such as fine clothing, watches, or expensive liquor and vacation related costs. These are simply those services and goods costs which an earner may choose to pay for according to their personal discretion.

When economic conditions warrant, both businesses and households may find that they have to reduce their outlays as revenues and incomes go down. This is why it is important to have a thorough understanding of discretionary expenses before hand. When these are separately broken out on paper or a spreadsheet, then businesses and consumer decision makers can quickly and easily ascertain what expenses can be lowered or cut altogether.

A helpful technique for budgeting lies in ranking those discretionary expenses by their order of relative importance. This could be done by putting the least important at the top of the list and continuing on down to most important. When business income reduction or a cut back in hours on the job occurs causing businesses or households to slash expenses, then it is easy for the spending decision makers to choose which expenses can and should be cut first.

It is also to keep in mind that there are differences between what businesses and consumers consider to be discretionary in nature. Families which have two cars will likely have two car payments. They may think that the two cars are necessities and not discretionary. The truth is different. In an emergency, they could manage with only the one car in many cases. When times become hard and a job is lost, the family can decide the second car is actually discretionary and not essential. This way, they can sell the second vehicle to remove the second payment overhead from the family or household budget.

Distressed Assets

Distressed assets are assets that a company or individual has been forced to place for sale at a significant discount to the acquired or actual value. This usually happens as the owner has no choice but to sell the asset to raise cash. Several different reasons might exist for why this is the case. These include excessive debt levels, bankruptcy, and regulatory requirements. Even debt can be put on sale at an amount that is lower than its face value. When this happens, it is known as distressed debt.

Although there are various types of distressed assets offered for sale, among the most common in the wake of 2007-2010's financial crisis and Great Recession are non performing loans on houses or foreclosures on mortgaged properties. Investors of all sizes are able to take advantage of such distressed assets in property by availing themselves of a homeowner's lack of ability to meet the mandatory mortgage payments or of his or her critical requirements for cash. In situations like this, such homeowners will consent much of the time to selling the property for a substantial discount in order to achieve a fast sale.

In the past, banks dealt with such distressed asset mortgages almost entirely themselves. As a result of the American banks still repairing their heavily damaged balance sheets from the countless write offs and over leveraging that they engaged in over the past five to ten years, they can not keep up any longer with the enormous number of foreclosures on their books. This leaves them with little choice but to have to sell some of their mortgage property asserts at massive discounts to actual value in order to be able to create quick cash flow.

The end result is that distressed assets can present a potentially profitable investment opportunity for you. The still ongoing crisis in global liquidity and credit has banks selling mortgages to individual, as well as to large, investors at significant discounts. Such discounts to perceived value would never occur in the days of normalized conditions in the mortgage and credit market place.

This means that investors are currently able to purchase distressed home assets with discounts amounting to as much as 72.5%. With as little as $100,000, smaller investors are able to get involved with this efficient and potentially lucrative investment strategy. Professional management teams are available to help small investors realize appropriate exit strategies whose goal is to generate an impressive 20% return on investment per year.

Purchasing distressed assets such as homes in mortgage payment trouble can offer ethical options and benefits as well. Investors are able to restructure the debt and payments of the home owner in such a way that distressed home owners are able to afford the new payments. This lets the troubled home owners stay in their houses so long as the investor owns the mortgage and the home owner is able to work with the newly arranged payment schedule.

Distressed assets of companies include many different types of assets. These might be commercial office buildings, commercial jets, and even factories and equipment sold at substantial discounts to real value. Many times, other corporations are able to acquire these distressed assets for their own uses at fantastic prices.

Due Diligence

The phrase due diligence is utilized to discuss a wide variety of legal obligations, assignments, investigations, and reports. These all are practiced in business, manufacturing and law. The most commonly used version of the phrase has to do with businesses.

In business, the concept of due diligence pertains to the process gone through by venture capitalists in advance of pouring funding into a start up company. Also involved with this are investigations that continue later into the ways that the monies are being spent. Large companies similarly engage in such due diligence before making the decision to buy out a smaller company.

Venture capitalists practice a particular brand of due diligence that involves researching the present and past players and structures of the firm that is looking for venture funding. Venture capitalists are careful about putting money into firms that do not feature principals who showcase either a track record that is well proven or at least impressive credentials.

Such a due diligence investigation could be stricter or more relaxed based on the prevailing amount of caution held by the investment community at any given time. With most venture capitalist firms, there will be more than a dozen investigators employed who spend their time investigating particular information on the personal histories of the corporation's personnel. This task has become far easier than ever before thanks to the rise of the Internet and all of the subsequent access to information that is now available. Looking into an individual's experience and associations is now far quicker and more convenient.

Due diligence is also used for background checks. When venture capitalist decision makers make up their mind concerning the prospective firm, they will order these done. Most of the time, such venture capitalist partners will want to give funds to individuals that they either feel confident can be trusted, or to whom they have disbursed funds before with other ventures.

Despite the practice of due diligence, it does not guarantee that the investment will not fail. Companies that are comprised of successful proven people with tremendous educational backgrounds and practical experience still fail all of the time because of competition that no one foresaw coming, difficult conditions in the market, or even technical difficulties with products.

Due diligence involves a different understanding from one company to the next firm. Within the business of manufacturing, some environmental protections have to be taken. These are checked out in the due diligence report having to do with environmental site assessments. Such a report contains specifications in a checklist, as well as available sections for commentary.

Due diligence is also used by law firms concerning care that should be taken by companies or individuals in a particular scenario. An example of this might be a company making certain that their product was thoroughly checked out in advance of selling it and then finding out that it might be poisonous or harmful in strangling incidents. Should they not do this due diligence, then they may be charged with criminal negligence.

Earnings Per Share (EPS)

Earnings per share refer to the given total of earnings that a company has for every share of the firm's stock that is outstanding. There are several formulas for calculating earnings per share. These depend on which segment of earnings are being considered. The FASB, or Financial Accounting Standards Board, makes corporations report such earnings per share on their income statement for all of the major components of such statements including discontinued operations, continuing operations, extraordinary items, and net income.

To figure up the basic net earnings per share formula, you only have to divide the profit for the year by the average number of common shares of stock. With discontinued operations, it is only a matter of taking the discontinued operations income and dividing it by the average number of common stock shares outstanding. Continuing operations earnings per share equal the continuing operations income over the average number of common shares. Extraordinary items works with the income from extraordinary items and divides it by the weighted average number of common shares.

Besides the basic earnings per share numbers, there are three different types of earnings per share. Last year's earning per share are the Trailing EPS. These are the only completely known earnings for a company. The Current earnings per share are the ones for this year. These are partially projections in the end until the last quarterly numbers are released. Finally, Forward earnings per share are earnings numbers for the future. These are entirely based on predictions.

Earnings per share calculations do not take into account preferred dividends on categories besides net income and continued operations. Such continuing operations and even net income earnings per share calculations turn out to be more complex as preferred share dividends are taken off of the top of net income before the earnings per share is actually calculated. Since preferred stock shares have the right to income payments ahead of common stock payments, any money that is given out as preferred dividends is cash which can not be considered to be potentially available for giving out to every share of the commonly held stock.

Preferred dividends for the present year are generally the only ones that are taken off of such income. There is a prevalent exception to this. If preferred shares prove to be cumulative then this means that dividends for the entire year are taken off, regardless of if they have been declared yet or not. Dividends that the company is behind on paying are not contemplated when the earnings per share is calculated.

Earnings per share as a financial measuring stick for a company are extremely important. In theory, this forms the underlying basis for the value of the stock in question. Another critical measurement of stock price is price to earnings value, also known as the PE ratio. This PE ratio is determined by taking the earnings per share and dividing them into the price of the stock. Earnings per share are useful in measuring up one corporation against another one, if they are involved in the same business segment or industry. They do not tell you if the stock is a good buy or not. They also do not reveal what the overall market thinks about the company. This is where the PE ratio is more useful.

Employees

Employees are individuals who work in the service of a business endeavor or trade. They do this by contributing their expertise, abilities, and labor to another individual's small business, a corporation, for the government, or in their own self employed business. Employees are also a critical component of the factors of production that include land, capital, and labor. In this capacity, they contribute the labor to a business enterprise.

In particular, an employee proves to be an individual who is engaged by some employer in order to perform a specific job or task. Within the majority of advanced nations and their economies, this word pertains to a specifically spelled out relationship that is established between companies and individual persons. This relationship is markedly different from that of a client or customer.

Attaining the status of employee generally results from undergoing a job interview with a certain business or corporation. Assuming that the person in question matches up well with the organization and their position, then she or he is made a formal employment offer for a given initial salary and place in the company. Such a person then attains all of the privileges, responsibilities, and rights as other employees. These commonly include vacation days and medical insurance benefits. Human Resource departments typically manage the actual relationships between such employees and major companies. This department works with new employees' coming on board and integrating into the organization, as well as handling the set up of their new benefits to which they are entitled. HR departments also commonly resolve any problems or grievances that employees experience.

Employees may group themselves into labor unions that can come to represent the positions and demands of the majority of an organization's work force. These labor unions are then capable of bargaining as a whole on behalf of the employees with a company's management. They do this to make demands for the members concerning payroll, benefits, and working conditions.

Employers are quick to point out that these offers of employment never assure employment for any future specified amount of time. Either the employer or the employee is capable of ending this particular relationship whenever it suits them. This capability is known as at will employment. Many professions expect a two week notice when an individual employee quits his or her job. This is a customary courtesy that the law does not require. It may be necessary in order to obtain a satisfactory job reference for future employment opportunities.

Equity Securities

Equity securities prove to be those asset classes which feature shares of stock in a given corporation. Investors hold these as reported by a company's official balance sheet. Corporations issue such securities in an effort to raise business capital via the financial markets. They use this money for significant company life events, such as for product development, merger and acquisition activity, or internal expansion. The funds are seldom for daily operating needs.

When investors buy equity securities, they gain a partial stake in the underlying firm. This is a primary alternative to turning to the bond markets to borrow money in taking on debt via the publicly traded bond markets. When a company first issues such equity securities, this is called an IPO initial public offering. Companies often raise enormous amounts of cash in this means, since investors are always hunting for new stock issues that will enable them to possess a part of a new and exciting opportunity.

The total number of shares that an IPO released varies wildly. It comes down to the amounts which the companies obtain permission to issue in their financial documents which they file with the regulatory overseer for their area. Corporations are allowed to sell a specific amount of stock shares in a given price range on the actual IPO day. After these shares have been dealt out to the public via the financial markets, the price of their equity will go up and down on the stock markets every trading day. This movement all depends on the perception of investors and the accompanying demand for the shares on any given day.

It is not common for such a firm to issue its entire inventory of available stock shares in a single offering. Rather than do this, they commonly reserve a certain quantity of shares to be issued at a later date in a second offering. This is called a follow on offering or secondary offering. The management of a company would elect to do this as they know they will likely need to raise fresh additional capital in the future in order to pay for hoped for expansionary plans.

When corporations continue to issue out their equity securities via the financial exchanges there is a downside for the existing shareholders and company investors. As additional shares are available to be bought, the pre-existing stake holders have their equity stake diluted as a percentage of the total. As an example, a major share holder could possess a huge quantity of shares that equate to fully 10 percent of all outstanding company shares which can be traded. Should the company choose to boost the total number of shares which are tradable, the equity of the shareholders will immediately drop in terms of the percentage ownership of all available shares.

The main alternative to issuing equity securities lies in issuing debt securities These publicly issued bonds offered via the bond markets by a company (or even government) raise money by taking on debt which must be repaid one day, known as the maturity date. Investors who buy debt instruments like these become de facto creditors of the bond issuing entities. The main disadvantage to such issuance in debt is that the company issuing has to provide continuous interest payments to the bond holders throughout the life of the bond contract. The company is able to maintain its ownership in itself in exchange for this trade off of interest payments.

European Investment Bank (EIB)

The European Investment Bank proves to be the bank of the European Union. As such it is the one and only bank which is both representing the EU member states' interests and also owned by the same member countries. This EIB works hand in glove with the other institutions of the European Union in order to carry out the common EU policies.

This European Investment Bank turns out to be the biggest multilateral lender and borrower on the planet. It delivers finance via loans and joint ventures as well as expertise to support projects of sustainable investments. While over 90 percent of the bank's projects remain in Europe, they are still a substantially large investor throughout the globe.

The European Investment Bank betters the quality of life for individuals within and without the continent of Europe by offering expertise and finance on projects which encourage SME's (small to medium enterprises), infrastructure, innovation, and climate action. Their enormous and far flung enterprises in areas of lending, blending, and advisory services work for the good of EU residents and citizens, along with residents of numerous countries which are not a part of the European Union.

Lending is the overwhelming center of activity for the European Investment Bank. By far the greatest share of the bank's financing occurs via loans. They do also provide microfinance, guarantees, and equity investment, among other types of financing. The bank is able to harness their vast financial resources in order to borrow money on the world markets at extremely competitive rates. They then deliver these cost savings to those projects which they deem to be economically practical and which foster the objectives of EU policy.

Lending accounts for nearly 90 percent of all their financial commitments. The European Investment Bank actually lends money to clients of all sizes and purposes in order to encourage jobs and sustainable growth. The support of this well-regarded institution tends to attract other investors to the projects. Such projects must be over 25 million Euros in order to qualify for a loan. They also facilitate intermediated loans through local area banks.

With their venture capital program, they assist fund managers to invest capital in growth area SME's and high technology companies. Microfinance they offer for both fund and equity investments as well.

Blending is the tool whereby the European Investment Bank helps to release funding from other financial sources by collaborating on a project. This support especially comes out of the EU budget. When blended along with loans, it helps to ensure a fully financed package of investment in a given project.

The EIB offers structured finance to give support to high priority projects. Guarantees ensure that a good project will be able to bring in sufficient new investment from other partners. Project bonds help to unlock funding for infrastructure projects. The InnovFin initiative delivers innovators EU based finance. The bank also partners with donors in trust funds. They support transport infrastructure and the JEREMIE project which delivers financial engineering and flexible finance to SME enterprises.

Other blending programs include ESIF Financial Instruments, the JESSICA program which supports urban development, the Private Finance for Energy Efficiency (PF4EE) program, and the Mutual Reliance Initiative offering efficient partnerships for development and growth.
Blending programs also include the Natural Capital Financing Facility to combine the bank's financing with that of the European Commission as part of the LIFE Program to assist climate and environmental actions. An interesting last blending program proves to be the Risk Capital Facility for the Southern Neighborhood. This gives access to debt and equity financing for SMEs found throughout the Mediterranean regions. Its goal is to foster growth which is inclusive, job creation in the private sector, and development in the private sector.

Advising services provide technical assistance and expertise in the form of project and administrative management capabilities. This helps to bring in other investment. Both pubic authorities and private companies are able to rely on the technical and financial experience of the European Investment Advisory Hub to make sure the entity obtains the best people needed for a given project.

Fed Funds Rate

Fed Funds Rate refers to the most key interest rate benchmark in the United States. Such a benchmark rate is the one which the banks charge one another in order to borrow money from each other overnight. The Federal Reserve similarly deploys this rate as a tool in order to meaningfully impact monetary policy within the country. This is not the only benchmark rate in America today, yet it has no rival for importance.

The way the Federal Reserve is able to influence banks with it is somewhat complicated. The commercial banks must maintain a minimum level of money either in cash funds or with their particular regional branch of the Federal Reserve on deposit. The idea behind this is that it allows banks to meet customer withdrawals from their current accounts, including both checking and savings.

Sensible banks hold more than this bare minimum. They keep an excess of the reserves that the regulations and rules pertaining to the banking universe require. These are appropriately referred to as excess reserves. It is such excess reserves that the Fed Funds Rate directly affects.

As the better prepared banks keep plenty of excess reserves available, they are able to overnight loan out to the less prepared banks so that they can end business day operations at their legally required minimum obligation. This unsecured overnight loan occurs at the Fed Funds Rate. It represents the effective rate that the lending bank will charge the borrowing bank.

In nearly all cases, this Fed Funds Rate proves to be the lowest practical interest rate in the nation. Since the financial crisis, it has remained at slightly higher than zero percent. The Federal Reserve began increasing it with their first rate hike in December of 2015, both slowly and gradually.

This rate matters for more reasons than just the price at which a lending bank will charge a borrowing bank to utilize its excess reserves. The reason is that the Federal Reserve is able to set their monetary policy with the rate. As an example, they might decide they need to cut the effective rate of unemployment in the U.S. This is one of their two reasons for existing (along with keeping inflation low). In order to increase employment opportunities, the Fed will push down the Fed Funds Rate through purchasing securities off of commercial banks. As bank reserves go up, the price for them declines. This is their means for pushing down the federal funds rate.

A lower Fed Funds Rate means that banks try to find better opportunities to engage their excess reserves. They might do this by loaning out the money to individuals who seek to purchase a house. They could also lend the cash to companies interested in expanding their business. Either of these actions will boost the economy in some meaningful way. A more active economy will create more jobs and drive down the unemployment rate.

Besides this, the banks also employ the Fed Funds Rate as their basing benchmark from which they determine their other key interest rates. Once the Federal Reserve boosted their federal funds rate target back in December of 2016 as an example, each of the main banks in the country instantly increased their prime loan lending rates. These represent those rates which they offer to their best customers who are extremely creditworthy. The best customers are usually the large and economically powerful MNC multinational corporations.

This means that the effective Fed Funds Rate is not simply the one that the banks are paying each other when they borrow excess reserves from one another. Instead, it has a dramatic and literal connection to the rate of interest any individual will pay for a car loan, home equity loan or line of credit, and mortgage. It also impacts the price that companies will pay to build and grow their business using bank loans.

Financial Statement

Financial statements are official records of a business' or personal financial activity. With businesses, financial statements present any and all pertinent financial activity as usable information. They do this in a clear, organized, and simple to comprehend way.

Financial statements are commonly comprised of four different types of financial accounts that come with an analysis and discussion provided by the company's management. The Balance sheet is the first of these. It is known by several other names, including statement of financial condition, or statement of financial position. The balance sheet details will outline a corporation's ownership equity, liabilities, and assets on a particular date. This will give a good picture of the general strength and position of the company.

Financial statements similarly include income statements. These can also be called Profit and Loss statements too. They outline numerous important pieces of company information, such as corporate expenses, income, and profits made in a certain time period. This statement explains all of the relevant financial details to the business' operation. Sales and all associated expenses are included under this category. This section of the financial statement proves to be the nuts and bolts of the whole document. It provides a snap shot of the company's ability to generate sales and turn profits.

A statement of cash flow is also a part of a complete financial statement. As its name implies, this section will share all of the details regarding the company's activities pertaining to cash flow. The most important ones that will be outlined include operating cash flow, financing, and investing endeavors.

The last element of a financial statement includes the statement of retained earnings. This section of the document makes good on its name to detail any changes to a corporation's actual retained earnings for the period that is being reported. These four sections of a financial statement are all combined together to make the consolidated financial statement, once they are combined with the analysis and discussion of management.

With large multinational types of corporations, such financial statements are typically large and complicated, making them challenging to read and understand. To assist with readability, they may also come with a group of notes for the financial statement that also covers management's analysis and discussion. Such notes will go through all items listed on the four parts of the financial statement in more thorough detail. For many companies, these notes for financial statements have come to be deemed a critical component of good and complete financial statements.

Financial statements are used by several different groups of people who are looking at a company. Investors use them in order to determine if the company and its stocks or bonds make a sound investment with a chance of providing good returns on investments and profits in exchange for limited risks. Banks utilize these financial statements to decide if a company is a good credit risk for their loan dollars. Institutions and other groups that may be considering a cash infusion or buyout of the company use such financial statements to decide if the company is a viable investment or acquisition target.

Financing Terms

There are two different financing terms available for businesses. These are short term financing and long term financing. In today's economic environment following the financial collapse and Great Recession, many businesses require both types. The two types of financing involve more differences than only the time frames.

Short term financing is commonly utilized for the daily business operations' funding and needs. This is also known as working capital. The financing terms for these short term facilities commonly require the short term loans to be paid back in a year or less.

Long term financing is more often utilized for the upkeep or purchase of fixed asset types. This might include a building or machinery that a firm owns. The financing terms for long term loans are for periods of time that are greater than a year.

Among the short term financing means are bank loans, bank overdrafts, trade credit, and leasing. For individuals, bank overdrafts prove to be the most common means of short term finance, since their finance terms permit an individual to draw out a greater amount of money that the person has in the bank, up to a predetermined amount.

Trade credit is useful for small businesses who may require the ability to buy goods and services or supplies before they receive payments and incoming receipts. With such trade credit facilities, the finance terms are commonly from thirty to ninety days to pay the full balance.

Long term financing might also involve bank loans, as well as corporate bonds or mortgages. With corporate bonds, a company is borrowing money from investors and members of the public. The financing terms of these types of instruments commonly require periodic interest payments that are known as coupon payments. The principal is then repaid on the agreed upon day. Many corporate bonds also feature a recall option that allows a company to pay off its long term debts early. This might be of interest to such a firm if they feel that they can borrow the funds for less money elsewhere or with lower interest rates.

Mortgages are extremely long term financing options made available to individuals or consumers for the purchase of a house or commercial property. These financing terms commonly run to thirty years or longer. Mortgages involve complex calculations for figuring out payments that often involve property taxes, mortgage insurance, and loan repayments.

Financing terms can also relate to the specifics of a particular loan, mortgage, or credit facility. They would spell out the interest rate, due dates of payments, and number of payments anticipated. In many cases, they would also specify the amount of interest that would be paid over the course of the loan or credit facility, as well as the penalties for not making the payments on time.

Fire Sale

A fire sale is a phrase with a variety of interesting meanings. The term originated in reference to the reduced sales price for goods which were damaged in a fire of a shop or business. Since then, it has come to refer to any event which forces a business to move its assets or inventory goods for prices that are substantially discounted. The reason the business would be forced to engage in such a practice is because they are in a bind through some type of serious and often-times fatal financial distress.

Where financial markets are concerned, the phrase fire sale also refers to any securities (stocks, bonds, or other financial instruments and investments) which trade at a deep discount to their intrinsic value. This could occur in extended and painful bear market phases in the equities markets.

There are a number of examples which help to clarify the several different meanings of this concept of a fire sale. Take a department store as a prime example. When the department store company has to close its doors because of a bankruptcy event, the store might offer such a sale. In this specific scenario, the department store will offer its inventory of goods at what would normally be considered ridiculously low prices.

They do this so that they can liquidate the entirety of their in stock inventory. Since the store is closing up for good, they must be rid of each item in the store's inventory. The only means of effectively accomplishing this lies in providing prices so drastically reduced that bargain hunters will be lured in to purchase the stock. When the prices offered on the merchandise are so good as to be irresistible, then this qualifies as a fire sale.

Where securities are concerned, there are always examples of a fire sale of a given stock issue. Any time a particular equity security sells for far less than the value it is perceived to be worth, this qualifies as such a sale. Look at a clear example to consider. When the Dow Jones Industrial Average cratered by a full thousand points within the day, Proctor and Gamble (ticker symbol PG) crashed and burned by a quarter of its value on a temporary basis. This led investors and analysts to declare that there had been a real fire sale on the share of Proctor and Gamble that particular day.

In this particular scenario, the phrase for this kind of a sale signifies that the asset in question possesses significantly greater value than the price for which its owner is suddenly willing to sell it.

These stock or bond securities which appear to be offered for this dramatic sale often provide an appealing risk to reward payoff possibility for the types of buyers known as value investors. This is because the asset is not likely to experience significantly further deterioration in valuation, yet the profit potential to the upside could possible prove to be impressive. The truth is that there is no single set of metrics for valuing whether or not a particular stock is actually selling for a ridiculously low price. One factor that many analysts can agree on is that if a stock is being valued at multiple year lows in the price, then it is generally considered to be a huge bargain.

As an example, stocks which are trading continuously for 14 times earning multiples would likely be fire sales when they trade for a far lower multiple of earnings of a mere seven. For this to be true in all scenarios though, the fundamentals for the given company and its stock must remain more or less unchanged. In other words, they can not simply have deteriorated appreciably in the meanwhile.

Fitch Group

The Fitch Group is the parent of four subsidiary companies. The original composite member of the group is Fitch Ratings. As the smallest of the Big Three agencies for credit ratings, Fitch has larger, more pervasive rivals in Standard & Poor's and Moody's. The United States SEC Securities and Exchange Commission set out its list of the three nationally accepted statistical ratings organizations, or NRSRO's, back in 1975.

The Fitch Group is headquartered jointly in New York City in the United States and in London, Great Britain. The company is majority held by the Hearst Corporation, which controls 80 percent of the group since it acquired an additional 30 percent interest in the worldwide ratings agency back on December 12th of 2014. This transaction equated to $1.965 billion. Hearst had controlled half of the group before this once acquired its original stake back in 2006. The balance 20 percent of the Fitch Group is held by French company FIMALAC, which still controls 50 percent of all board voting rights through 2020.

The company became founded on December 24th of 1914 by John Knowles Fitch in New York City when he named it the Fitch Publishing Company. Over 80 years later, the smallest of the big three credit ratings agencies merged with IBCA of London in December of 1997. Fitch Group expanded still more when it made two additional acquisitions in the year 2000 - Thomson Financial Bank Watch in December and Duff & Phelps Credit Rating Co. in April. Thanks to acquisitions such as these, the company has been able to finally position itself in the role of a tie breaker between the varying ratings of Moody's and Standard & Poor's, which sometimes have unequal but similar-scaled ratings.

Today's Fitch Group proves to be a worldwide leader of services in financial information that boasts impressive operations spanning over 30 different nations. The group is made up of four divisions including Fitch Ratings, Fitch Solutions, BMI Research, and Fitch Learning.

Fitch Ratings is the original core component of the company which evolved from the earliest incarnation of the company Fitch Publishing. It is a leader around the world in credit research and ratings. The division is committed to delivering more than only independent perspectives on its opinions of credit. Fitch Ratings also provides truly international points of view based on its credit market experience and local expertise. Over a century of industry-leading growth for investors who sought out the company's professional and trusted opinion has been the result. The group provides comprehensive ratings on emerging markets, corporate finance, financial institutions, insurance, project and infrastructure finance, sovereign debt ratings, public finances, and structured financial product offerings.

Fitch Solutions turns out to be an industry leader in the provision of credit market data, risk services, and analytical tools for the worldwide financial industry. The company delivers its own market-centric content as well as acting as distributing agent for its sister group Fitch Ratings in a range of inventive platforms. It specializes in fundamental financial data, ratings & research, the proprietary Fitch Connect service, and analytics.

BMI Research is the group's entirely independently based creator and distributor of both industry and nation analysis. This involves a unique holistic approach that combines analysis of industry, macroeconomic trends, and financial markets together. They concentrate their specialty on frontier and emerging markets in what they call Total Analysis. BMI maintains offices and operations in New York, South Africa, and Singapore. They deliver information on 200 international markets across 24 different industries. This includes specializations in country risk, industry reports, and the financial markets.

Fitch Learning is the group's professional and training operation. They provide regulatory training, financial training classes, specifically tailored training, and qualifications in CISI, CQF, and CFA for their own employees and those of other corporations around the globe. This arm of the group has important centers in London, New York, Hong Kong, Singapore, and Dubai.

Fixed Income

Fixed Income refers to the kind of budgeting and investing style that delivers periodic income and actual returns back to the owners of the investments. This income goes out in generally predictable amounts in frequent and anticipated intervals. The investors who flock to fixed income investments are usually retirees. They count on such periodic returns from investments to give them a stable and regular stream of income. Thanks to the dependable returns they provide, this type of investment is heavily preferred by the demographic of older investors.

Fixed income also defines a style of investing whose goal is to provide a general stream of stable and fixed income. Where individual lifestyles are concerned, it also relates to the income of a specific household or a particular individual. Mutual funds can be of this type of investing strategy. This portion of the funds will be invested in vehicles that provide low risk and which pay out interest or dividends. Bonds or mutual funds containing bonds are classic examples of these kinds of investments.

It is true that fixed income is most popular with retirees for a good reason. At this point in these investors' lives, they need to count on both predictable and stable returns and regular income. It is the income sources such as investment returns, pensions, Social Security payouts, annuities, and other funds that generate the more or less same level of income retired individuals find necessary to sustain a given lifestyle from year to year. This is the reason that retirees are also a good explanation of the phrase fixed income. Their income is fixed, so they can not absorb additional costs and increases in living expenses.

Because the point of overall fixed income investment strategy is for guaranteeing a dependable stream of income, these investment fund advisors generally favor dividend yielding mutual funds, bonds, certificates of deposit, differing kinds of annuities, and money market funds.

Bonds still remain among the most common and popular of these fixed income investments today. Large corporations, local governments like municipalities and counties, state and provincial governments, and national governments all issue such bonds of different types. These investments provide a nice income for not only retirees but also other investors who are on the lookout for a diversified portfolio. The percentages of a portfolio dedicated to fixed income will vary depending on the individual investor's needs and preference (or tolerance) for risk.

As an example, an investor could allocate a portfolio to the following fixed income categories. They might choose 50 percent to investment grade bonds, 20 percent to high yield bonds, 15 percent to Treasuries, and 15 percent to international bonds. Those products which are considered to be riskier, like longer maturity instruments and junk rated bonds, should always be a small percentage of the total portfolio in question. Naturally bonds which are riskier will pay a higher amount of interest or coupon rate since there is a greater chance of risk.

Besides bond yields, investors who are seeking income that is fixed have other choices for returns. There are interest paying investments like CDs and money market funds available.

Examples of concerns that affect fixed income instruments are important to consider. Borrowers can default on bonds, even those these are generally considered to be safe investments (though junk bonds are usually not). There are also exchange rate risks involved with international bonds. Longer maturity date fixed investments are also subject to a risk of interest rates going up over time, which could reduce the asset value of the underlying instrument. This is because where bonds are concerned interest rates and values are inversely correlated.

Franchise

A franchise can be defined in many ways. The definition from the International Franchise Association describes franchising as a means to expand a business so that goods and services can be distributed more effectively via a licensing relationship. The word itself legally means a specific kind of license. Ultimately, franchising refers to the personal relationship which a franchisor maintains with its franchisees.

In this arrangement, the franchisor licenses out its trade name as well as its operating methods, or systematic way of doing business, to a particular franchisee. In exchange for this arrangement, the franchisee pledges to run the business as per the terms of this license. The operating method here refers to the franchisor's system and way of doing business.

Franchisors guarantee their franchisees will have their support and help. They also maintain a certain level of control over specific parts of the franchisee business. This is critical for the franchise owner to safeguard its intellectual property rights as well as to be certain that the franchisee keeps to the guidelines of the brand itself. The quid pro quo of this is that the franchisee typically delivers a one time start up fee (known as the franchise fee) to the franchisor. The franchisees also pay a royalty fee to the franchisor, which is periodic and continuous. This enables the franchisee to utilize the franchisor's operating system and trade name.

The franchisor itself carries little responsibility for involvement in the daily management of the business of the franchisee. This is because franchisees exist as independent operators. Neither are they joint employers with their franchisors. This gives the franchisees a free hand in hiring employees, paying them according to their wishes, scheduling their shifts as they see fit, arranging their employment rules and practices, and even disciplining their own employees, all without requiring any approval from their franchisor. However, the uniforms which the employees wear will be stipulated by the brand and operating system of the franchisor.

Franchising is about a contractually defined relationship between the two parties. The franchisees and franchisor will share the brand in common. Despite this, both are distinctly separate businesses in both real terms and legally. The role of the franchisor is simply to build up its business and brand as part of supporting the various franchisees. The part which the franchisees play is to operate and manage their own business according to the specific terms of the franchise agreements.

It is interesting that definitions of franchises range from one state to the next according to the various laws which different states enforce. Some states include among the various elements of franchising the responsibilities of the franchisor to deliver a marketing plan to its franchisees. Others insist that the franchisor maintain an interested community of the business jointly with the franchisee.

Business Format Franchises are the most readily recognizable types of these arrangements for the everyday individual. These relationships typically cover the whole of the business and its format, not only the products, services, and trade name of the franchisor in question. In this common type, franchisors are expected to give their franchisees training, operating manuals, standards for the brand, a marketing plan and strategy to carry it out, quality control monitoring, and more.

Examples of the idea make these distinctions clear. Pizza Hut does not license out pizzas or breadsticks. Burger King does not license out hamburgers or chicken sandwiches. The two mega franchise operations instead license out components of their intellectual property. In this case it includes both their business systems and their trade marks, or their ways of producing these food items and company-described premises and atmosphere.

The history of these and other brands demonstrates that both services and products have changed significantly over the decades. Among the various advantages to these types of business format franchises and their arrangements is that they have the flexibility to do so effectively.

Today there exist numerous kinds of franchises throughout a constantly expanding array of industries and market segments in not only the United States and Canada but around the globe. Estimates state that more than 120 separate industries utilize the concept and practices of franchising now. The greatest share of franchising by far is still the food and restaurants businesses. Nowadays even medical services and home based health care rely on franchising though.

Franchise Model

Franchises are businesses where the owners sell the rights of their business to third parties. The owners of the franchise are known as franchisors. The third party operators who buy the rights are called franchisees. The franchise model is the precise way the business is run to insure uniformity among the different regional or national franchise outlets.

This model of business offers advantages to the sellers and the buyers of the franchise. Franchisors who sell their rights gain the ability to grow their business brand faster than they might with their own capital or by using the help of lenders or investors. They are able to harness other individuals' money to build up the business footprint faster than they can alone. They still maintain control over the brand.

Franchisors receive both an upfront franchise fee and continuous royalties. They avoid the deadlines of loan repayments with this model. With the royalties and fees that the franchisors gain, they are able to run the corporate headquarters operations, advertise and market the business brand, support and train their franchisees, build up their brand in the industry, and make improvements on the service or products that their business provides.

Franchisees also gain many benefits. Their franchise has a greater likelihood of succeeding than if they start up their own business. This is evident in many ways. They receive upfront training and continuous support. The time to open is less. Buyers also receive the recognition of a brand that is known, help in finding the best site for the new location, lesser costs because of group purchasing power, and better advertising exposure through regional and national campaigns.

Besides this, they receive leads that are generated by call centers and websites, the established franchise model, and moral support and counsel from fellow franchisee peers. A more recent benefit for franchisees pertains to help getting funding secured for startup and ongoing operation costs.

The model has been wildly successful particularly with nationally known franchises such as McDonald's, Subway, and Panerra Bread. Yet there are still downsides to the franchise model. These disadvantages apply to franchisees. Most importantly, they have little independence. This is evident from their services and goods they provide to franchise wide promotions that might not be effective in their own individual market.

Franchisees will have to utilize the company colors and approved paint colors on their walls. They can be made to redesign their units at significant expense. Most dangerous of all is the possibility that the franchise transforms after the franchisee signs a 10 to 15 year long contract. The ownership or management could completely change and force the brand to go in a different direction that the franchisee does not like or at all want.

The franchise model is all about following the system. This idea is central to the success of a franchisee's efforts. The reason that a franchisee purchases the franchisor's model and system is because they have confidence in it. Franchisees feel they can succeed and make money if they follow the system perfectly.

A good franchisor considers appropriate regional variations and suggestions for some changes. They also know that if they leave the system without gaining approval from the franchisor first, they may violate the franchise agreement. This could cause them to have their rights to use the franchisor's name and business model revoked.

Franchisees are also required to keep confidential any trade secrets or proprietary methods of business. They are also made to sign and abide by a non-compete clause agreement.

Free Market

Free Market is the term that refers to a system of exchange and trading that takes place voluntarily in a given economic jurisdiction. These markets have the characteristics of decentralization and spontaneous arrangements whereby the people involved are able to make real economic choices with their money. No country in the world has a completely free market. The degree of its freedom depends heavily on the legal framework and political rules. In some nations where markets are centrally planned or at least tightly regulated by an oppressive government (such as in the pariah state of North Korea), the only free markets may be enormous black markets which the government can not or chooses not to control or shut down.

The phrase Free Market is often utilized in place of the French idea of laissez-faire forms of capitalism. This phrase translates to "hands off." When the majority of individuals and investors refer to free markets, they are describing economies where competition is relatively unhindered and transactions are done on a generally private basis between willing sellers and buyers. A better definition would be a market in which economic activity is voluntarily and not coerced or heavily restricted by oppressive governmental authority.

With this more inclusive definition, both voluntary socialism and laissez-faire capitalism are real examples of the free markets. It does not matter that the socialism involves public ownership of the factors of production. So long as a central government is not restricting or impeding the free exchange of goods and economic activity, it is still Free Market capitalism. Coercion can be allowed in free markets in the cases of mutually agreed to terms as part of voluntarily signed contracts. This is how tort law and lawsuits operate under free market capitalism, though legal cases are certainly coercive obstructions to free economic activity.

It is the free market that makes it possible for goods from all across the globe to be made available to consumers in different countries. It similarly provides the greatest possible opportunities to entrepreneurs and business people. They put their personal capital at risk in order to meet the desires (both now and in the future) of the many global consumers as effectively and price-efficiently as they can. These free markets allow for savings and investment to produce capital goods while boosting the productivity of the workers (and hopefully their wages as well). It usually increases the standard of living of the employees as part of the process. Freely competing markets encourage and foster technological process and innovation which helps the inventors to satisfy the future desires of consumers across the world in creative and groundbreaking new ways.

Free markets allow for and cause the development of financial markets over time. Such markets provide for the finance and capital needs of those individuals and businesses which require greater capital resources for their business ventures than they can fund alone. While some businesses may save money through thriftiness, others actually deploy their savings in an effort to make money by expanding or incubating a new business. Securities can then be traded on secondary markets to encourage both activities.

As an example, individuals and investors who save are able to sink their resources into either the bonds or stocks of corporations. When they buy bonds, investors are providing their current savings to the businesses and entrepreneurs in exchange for the contractual agreement to repay these savings along with interest. When they purchase stocks, they are selling their savings in exchange for future claims on earnings not yet realized by the corporation.

There are many constraints that central governing authorities and regulating agencies impose on the free markets. These all come with either a verbal or implied threat of force if they are not heeded. Some of these constraints include taxation, licensing requirements, price and wage controls, quotas on exports or production, employee hiring regulations, sourcing of goods regulations, fixed exchange rates, and general regulations of many different kinds. When these restrictions become too repressive, voluntary exchange usually still occurs outside the government's knowledge in a black market. The problems with such markets is that oligopolies and monopolies often form in these underground free markets as competition is often ineffective and the prices are heavily impacted.

Global Debt

Global debt is an issue that has become especially troublesome since the financial crisis of 2007-2009. Eight years following this crash and Great Recession, the planet is experience a debt problem that has never before been seen in the whole history of the world.

Total debt outside of the financial sector has increased by more than double in real dollars since the century began through 2016. By 2015, it had climbed to over $152 trillion. This figure that includes the debt of governments, households, and non financial firms continues to grow.

Global debt levels as of October 2016 reached a record setting 225% of the entire gross domestic product for the globe, per the IMF's Fiscal Monitor semi annual publication. Roughly two thirds of the total non-financial firm debt is owed by the private sector of businesses and consumers. The balance nearly a third of the total is considered to be government public debt. While other measures have this percentage higher, the IMF claims that government debt is up to 85 percent of GDP versus the 70 percent seen in 2015.

This enormous amount of global debt has made the job of worldwide policy makers much more challenging. Central banks have found that their efforts to stimulate economies are diminishing. It is up to government fiscal policy to increase growth to try to keep up with rising global debt. So far, few countries have seen much success in these efforts.

The surge in global debt borrowing hails back to the private debt boom that occurred before the financial crisis in 2008. Corporations and consumer households within the world's advanced economies began to retrench after the crisis. Despite this, debt deleveraging did not proceed evenly and in other cases debts continued to rise. Bad debts of banks especially proved problematic. Many of these have wound up on the balance sheets of governments instead.

The low interest rate environment that followed the financial crisis also encouraged a rising tide of corporate debt in the emerging nation markets. Private debt levels were already dangerously high in advanced countries. Now they are also problematic in such important emerging economies as

Brazil and China. Both of these are rightly thought of as systemically critical in the world's financial system.

The problem with deciding how dangerous global debt has become is there is no consensus on what percentage of debt versus GDP is critical. It is well known that financial crises are related to an overabundance of private debt in developing and developed economies. Beyond this, research has demonstrated that higher levels of debt come with lower rates of growth, even though a financial crisis may be side stepped. The IMF has been warning especially about the need for deleveraging to happen in both the euro zone area and China.

There are two more problems associated with rising debt levels. As debt increase outpaces economic output growth, more government debt equals a greater level of state involvement in the overall economy. It also guarantees a higher tax rate and number of taxes for the future.

Besides this, debt has to be rolled over regularly. The repetition of having to auction debt creates a scenario where governments face a vote of confidence on a routine basis. Should a government fail to inspire enthusiasm for its debt auction as has happened with a number of euro zone governments in past years, then the erring nation plunges head long into serious crisis.

Good Debt

Good debt is debt that benefits a person or business to carry. Such good debts demonstrate both the creditworthiness and the responsibility of a borrower. They also create a good base to build on in the future. There are many examples of good debt, which stands in contrast to bad debt.

Good debts are typically those debts that are taken on to acquire an item or investment that only grows in value with time. Examples of this include things like real estate loans, schooling loans, home mortgages, business debt, and passive income investments. Each of these items could provide a significant and real advantage with time. Real estate could increase in value and be resold for profits.

Higher education commonly leads to greater amounts of earnings. Loans on homes are commonly wonderful for building credit and provide properties that serve as excellent collateral. Loans for businesses may result in profits earned from trade and sales. It is important to note that cars and other items are not included in these lists. This is simply because they lose value the moment that they are purchased and driven away.

Bad debts in contrast are those that result in higher interest rates and considerable deprecation of the items purchased with time. Goods that are for short time frame use and bought on credit are commonly considered to be bad debts. Since the item's life span will only decline with time, and the interest rates are typically high, no benefit is derived from purchasing these things with debt. A great number of such purchases rapidly decline in value, even after one use.

A significant benefit to good debts lies in the increase in cash flow that they commonly create. Properly structured good debts lead to tax advantages, to the ability to invest in still more assets that can produce cash, and to higher credit scores as well. Good debts that are paid on time furthermore build up a good financial base for the future. Good debts create cash flow, which stands in contrast to bad debts that do not.

Investments that produce passive income are among the best good debts. For example, purchasing an apartment building using debt will result in both income revenue and substantial tax deductions. This proves to be good debt, since although you are borrowing money, you are receiving passive income and gaining the ability to depreciate assets that can actually appreciate with time. On top of this, you are allowed to live there while you accrue all of these other benefits.

When considering a good debt, you should make certain that the income that the investment will provide is high enough to make the investment and the accompanying debt worth while. A number of experts offer advice on this. They suggest that not tying up in excess of twenty percent of your overall value in debt is a better practice. Higher debt levels than this can sound off warning bells with banks and other lenders.

Gross Income

Gross income can be several different things in the United States. In tax law for business, gross income signifies all proceeds realized from every source minus the cost of goods that have been sold. It is also used for individuals and pertains to all income earned from any and every kind of source.

As such, it is not simply cash that has been realized, but it can also be income received in kind, as property, or as services. For a taxpayer, gross income is commonly believed to be all of the monies and values received. Although most income is tallied into this figure, a few kinds of income are excluded deliberately.

For companies, individuals, trusts, estates, and others, gross income is necessary for figuring up the mandatory income taxes within the United States. Taxes are figured up using a taxable income number that starts with gross income and then subtracts permissible tax deductions. Taxes are then calculated based on the resulting taxable income.

Many different types of income are considered to be a part of the gross income category. Wages are the earnings for work performed payable as tips, salaries, and related income. Income made as a result of such personal service is always tallied up in a person's gross income. Gross profits made from selling an inventory of products are also considered gross income. Gross profits result from sales prices of items minus the cost of the goods actually sold.

All interest received is also considered to be a part of gross income. Dividends, along with distributions of capital gains from companies or mutual funds are similarly a part of gross income. Gains on property that has been disposed of are also tallied into the gross income total after the extra proceeds beyond the adjusted cost in the property is determined. Also included are royalties and rents from intangible and tangible items.

A number of other non traditional types of income are also considered to be a part of this. Pensions, income from life insurance, and annuities income are counted. So are alimony, child support, and other maintenance payments. Shares of partnership income that are distributed fall under this category. Even the proceeds from national and state tax refunds are considered to be gross income.

The Internal Revenue Service claims that such gross income includes all forms of income from any source of which they are derived. As such, gross income can result from any gains having to do with labor, capital, the two together, or profits having to do with the sale of anything or a capital asset. A notable exception to gross income includes gifts and inheritances. While these could be taxed under the category of estate taxes or gift taxes, they are not deemed by the IRS to be a part of gross income.

Gross Margin

Gross Margin is also known as gross profit margin. This concept represents a business formula that companies compute. It is best expressed as the firm's total revenue less its cots of goods sold which is then divided by the total revenue. This provides the answer as a percentage. In other words, Gross Margins are the percentage of revenues the corporations keep after paying their direct expenses of creating both their services and goods. Higher percentages mean a company keeps a larger amount of every dollar worth of sales. This greater amount of retained income provides it with more money for servicing debt, making new investments, retained earnings, and paying out dividends to shareholders.

Gross margin equates to the amount from every sales dollar that the firm is able to keep for their gross profits. Consider a concrete and tangible real world example to better understand this idea. If HSBC Bank has a gross margin in a quarter of 30 percent, then this means it keeps 30 cents from every dollar in revenue it creates. The other 70 cents would go into the Cost of Goods Sold (COGS) category. Since all of the bank's COGS are already considered, the other 30 cents per dollar in revenue may be applied to general overhead, paying down any debt, expenses on interest, and shareholder dividend distributions.

Corporations utilize this gross margin in order to ascertain how their costs of production are measuring up against their revenues. When a corporation's gross margin is declining, it will try to find ways to reduce its costs of suppliers and labor costs. The supplier costs can be slashed by finding alternative suppliers who will supply the goods at lower prices. The other solution is to try to raise the prices on the company goods and services so as to increase the value of the corporate sales revenues.

Another effective use of gross margins lies in predicting the amount of money which they will retain towards general operating costs. Companies with 45 percent gross margins know they will have to work with 45 cents on each dollar of revenue they collect in order cover their remaining administrative and operating costs. The measure also allows for firms to measure up their efficiency as a company. Investors and analysts are able to compare and contrast two or more corporations of varying sizes against one another with the metric as well.

Gross margin should never be erroneously confused with net profit margin. Gross margin simply considers the connection between the cost of goods sold and the sales revenue. On the other hand, net profit margin covers every expense a corporation has. Calculating up the net profit margins requires firms to start with their revenues and subtract out their cost of goods sold and other expenses. This includes sales rep wages, distribution of product costs, taxes, and various operating costs.

Another way of looking at the differences between the two related but still different concepts is that the gross profit margin allows firms to determine the level of their manufacturing operations' profitability. Alternatively the net profit margin assists firms in considering their level of all around profitability.

Consider another example for calculating up gross profit margin. If a company brings in two million dollars in sales revenue, it might spend $800,000 on its labor expenses and another $200,000 on the manufacturing inputs. Once these costs of goods sold of one million dollars are subtracted out, a full million dollars remains in total gross profits. When individuals take the gross profits and divide it by the total revenue, the result is 0.5. Turned into a percentage, this equals a gross profit margin of 50 percent.

Hedge Fund

A hedge fund is an investment fund which are commonly only open to a specific group of investors. These investors pay a large performance fee each year, commonly a certain percent of their funds under management, to the manager of the hedge fund. Hedge funds are very minimally regulated and are therefore are able to participate in a wide array of investments and investment strategies.

Literally every single hedge fund pursues its own strategy of investing that will establish the kinds of investments that it seeks. Hedge funds commonly go for a wide range of investments in which they may buy or sell short shares and positions. Stocks, commodities, and bonds are some of these asset classes with which they work.

As you would anticipate from the name, hedge funds typically try to offset some of the risks in their portfolios by employing a number of risk hedging strategies. These mostly revolve around the use of derivatives, or financial instruments with values that depend on anticipated price movements in the future of an asset to which they are linked, as well as short selling investments.

Most countries only allow certain types of wealthy and professional investors to open a hedge fund account. Regulators may not heavily oversee the activities of hedge funds, but they do govern who is allowed to participate. As a result, traditional investment funds' rules and regulations mostly do not apply to hedge funds.

Actual net asset values of hedge funds often tally into the many billions of dollars. The funds' gross assets held commonly prove to be massively higher as a result of their using leverage on their money invested. In particular niche markets like distressed debt, high yield ratings, and derivatives trading, hedge funds are the dominant players.

Investors get involved in hedge funds in search of higher than normal market returns. When times are good, many hedge funds yield even twenty percent annual investment returns. The nature of their hedging strategies is supposed to protect them from terrible losses, such as were seen in the financial crisis from 2007-2010.

The hedge fund industry is opaque and difficult to measure accurately. This is partially as a result of the significant expansion of the industry, as well as an inconsistent definition of what makes a hedge fund. Prior to the peak of hedge funds in the summer of 2008, it is believed that hedge funds might have overseen as much as two and a half trillion dollars. The credit crunch hit many hedge funds particularly hard, and their assets under management have declined sharply as a result of both losses, as well as requests for withdrawals by investors. In 2010, it is believed that hedge funds once again represent in excess of two trillion dollars in assets under management.

The largest hedge funds in the world are JP Morgan Chase, with over $53 billion under management; Bridgewater Associates, having more than $43 billion in assets under management; Paulson and Company, with more than $32 billion in assets; Brevan Howard that has greater than $27 billion in assets; and Soros Fund Management, which boasts around $27 billion in assets under management.

High Yield Bonds

High Yield Bonds turn out to be bonds that possess a lower credit rating and higher yield than those corporate, municipal, and sovereign government bonds which are of investment grade. Thanks to the greater risk of them defaulting, such bonds yield a higher return than the bonds which are qualified investment grade issues. Those companies that issue high yielding debt are usually capital intensive companies and startup firms that already possess higher debt ratios. Investors often refer to such bonds as junk bonds.

The two principal corporate rating credit agencies determine the breakdown of what qualifies as a High Yield Bond and what does not. When Moody's rates a bond with lower than a "Baa" rating, or Standard and Poor's (S&P) rates then with an under "BBB" rating, then they become known as junk bonds. At the same time, all of those bonds which enjoy higher ratings than these (or the same rating at least) investors will consider to be investment grade. There are credit ratings that cover such categories as presently in default, or "D." Those kinds of bonds holding "C" ratings and below also have high probabilities for defaulting. In order to compensate the investors who take them on for the significant risks they run of not receiving either their original principal back or accrued interest payments by the maturity date, the yields must be offered at extremely high interest rates.

Despite the negative label of "junk bond," these High Yield Bonds remain popular and heavily bought by global investors. The majority of these investors choose to diversify for safety sake by utilizing either a junk bond ETF exchange traded fund or a High Yield Bonds mutual fund. The spread between the yields on the higher yielding and investment grade types of bonds constantly fluctuates on the markets. The at the time condition of the global and national economies impacts this. Industry-specific and individual corporate events also play a part in the differences between the various kinds of bonds' interest rates.

In general though, High Yield Bonds' investors can count on receiving a good 150 to 300 basis points more in yield as measured against the investment quality bonds in any particular time frame. This is why mutual funds and ETFs make imminent sense as an effective means of gaining exposure to the greater yields without taking on the unnecessary risk of a single issuer's bonds defaulting and costing the investors all or most of their original investing principal.

In the last few years, various central bankers throughout the globe have decided to inject enormous amounts of liquidity into their individual economies so that credit will remain cheaply and easily available. This includes the European Central Bank, the U.S. Federal Reserve, and the Bank of Japan. It has created the side effect of causing borrowing costs to drop and lenders to experience significantly lower returns.

By February of 2016, an incredible $9 trillion in sovereign government debt bonds provided yields of only from zero percent to one percent. Seven trillion of the sovereign bonds delivered negative real yields once adjusted for anticipated levels of inflation. It means that holding such bonds cost investors money, or provided them a real losing return.

In typical economic environments, this would drive intelligent investors to competing markets that provide better return rates. Higher yield bond markets have stayed volatile though. Distressed debts which pay minimally a yield higher than 1,000 basis points greater than a comparably maturing Treasury bond were notably affected. Energy company high yielding debt bond prices collapsed by approximately 20 percent in 2015 as a consequence of the problems in the energy sector which resulted from plummeting energy prices.

High Yield Preferred Stocks

Preferred stocks are a special type of stocks that many companies issue. These types of stocks provide investors with a different level of ownership in a given company. A preferred stock holder obtains a higher priority on the earnings and assets of a company than a common stock holder would enjoy. These preferred stocks also pay a higher dividend that has to be given out before any dividends can be paid to the common stock holders.

As such, they represent a hybrid type of security on the stock markets. They are like common stocks in that they are bought and sold as stocks and represent ownership in a company. These stocks can also trade up and down in price like a common stock. Unlike a common stock, they do not come with any rights to vote for a company board of directors or items on a company ballot at the annual meeting.

They are also like bonds in that they pay a higher dividend that must be paid out unless the company lacks the earnings to pay these holders. In this way preferred stocks have elements of bonds with their fixed rate of dividends. Every preferred stock comes with its own unique details that are set when the company issues the stock.

Preferred stocks are often higher yielding issues. They are most commonly issued by companies that are in industries such as financials, real estate investment trusts, utilities, industrials, and conglomerates. Despite this higher yield that makes them like bonds, they can be traded on the major stock exchanges. They are typically found on exchanges including the NASDAQ and the New York Stock Exchange.

As preferred stocks are a type of equity legally, they show up as equity on any company balance sheet. Both common and preferred stock holders are owners in the company. There are several advantages to preferred stocks that investors like about them.

In the past, individual retail investors were less aware of preferred stocks, but this is changing. Part of the reason they have gained in popularity surrounds market volatility. As common stocks have seen wild price swings in recent years, investors have been looking for more stable instruments in which they can invest.

Preferred stocks fit this need as they tend to be more stable in price than do common stocks. With more baby boomers looking for investments that provide higher yields, this has brought preferred stocks into the spotlight. The retirees gain the advantage of better yields and the opportunity for the price to increase in the issues as well.

Preferred stocks are not new. They have existed from the time when modern day investing began. Institutional investors have known about and invested in them for many decades. Many individual investors did not because they lacked the information they required to select and trade them.

In the past, individuals did not have any lists of preferred stocks from which to pick. The information available was difficult to come up with before the Internet made this kind of information much more readily available. Now there are tools smaller individual investors can find that provide calendar searches for ex-dividend dates.

There are also screening filters that allow individuals to narrow down their search for the best high yielding dividend preferred stocks. Preferred stocks represent another way to diversify an investor's portfolio and earn higher yields on dividends at the same time.

Holdings

Holdings refer to the asset contents in a given portfolio which an entity or individual possesses. Pension funds and mutual funds are good examples of organizations that have holdings. These positions can include all sorts of different investment assets and classes. Among these are stocks, mutual funds, bonds, futures, options, ETF exchange traded funds, and private equity assets.

It is both the kinds and amounts of such holdings in any portfolios that determine how well-diversified the portfolio actually proves to be. Well-diversified portfolios often include various sectors of stocks, bonds from a range of maturities and companies, and a variety of other investments that do not correlate with either stocks or bonds. Alternatively, only a few positions in several stocks that come from only one sector would be indicative of poorly diversified portfolios.

It is actually the mix and amount of various asset classes in any portfolio that will substantially determine what its total rate of return will be. The biggest positions will exert a larger impact on the return of a portfolio than marginal or tinier holdings in such a portfolio will. Many investors make it a practice to closely scrutinize the lists of positions which the world's most successful money managers maintain in an effort to follow their trades.

Such investors try to imitate the trading prowess of these superior results money managers in a variety of ways. It might be the manager has purchased stocks, in which case the imitating investors will try to stake out a similar company position. If these managers sell out of a stake, the investors will similarly sell off their assets in the company. The problem with such a follower strategy is that there is often substantial lag time between that point where the money managers make their moves and when this information becomes public domain knowledge.

There is another variation on the idea of mutual funds, hedge funds, and pension funds. This is the concept of holding companies. Such organizations are groups where the investors organize their positions and assets as an LLC Limited Liability Company. The reasons for this are varied. It might be they wish to decrease their own risk exposure, pool their investment dollars with fellow investors, and/or reduce their taxes as much as possible. Such companies rarely operate their own businesses directly. Instead, they are generally only a vehicle utilized to own various investments and companies.

Probably the best-known example of such an LLC company is the internationally followed Berkshire Hathaway, Inc. This Warren Buffet-dominated Omaha, Nebraska- based corporation originally began as a clothing textiles' manufacturing firm. Over the last numbers of decades, the corporation has solely existed as Warren Buffet's personal vehicle to buy out, maintain, and sell out his numerous and wide-ranging investments in various companies. Among the greatest and most significant positions which Berkshire owns are large stakes in the Coca-Cola Company, Dairy Queen Inc, and their wholly controlled subsidiary GEICO Government Employees Insurance Company.

The simplest way to envision these holdings is to mentally picture a large bucket, which represents the mutual fund. Every rock within the bucket stands for an individual bond or stock position. When analysts add up all of the rocks (as stocks or bonds), this equals the aggregate numbers of all holdings.

Figuring out the best mix of these holdings is the challenge that mutual funds, pension funds, and hedge funds all grapple with on a regular basis. It all comes down to the type of fund which they represent. Those bond funds or index funds would anticipate having many positions. This could mean from hundreds to thousands of different bonds and stocks. With the majority of other funds, too many or too few positions is risky and dangerous. Those funds that hold merely 30 positions would be subject to extreme volatility and single stock risks. If they had 500 to 600 different stocks or bonds then the fund would be as large as many indices like the S&P 500.

Hostile Takeover

A hostile takeover refers to a type of acquisition which involves a buying company and a takeover target. Technically there is no strict difference between the concepts of friendly acquisition and hostile takeover. Yet the connotation is vastly different between the two. When the word takeover becomes used, it generally means that the target company is not a willing participant or is actively resisting. The target may oppose being bought out for a number of reasons. These could range from corporate tradition and pride to feeling an offer does not value them highly enough. Other companies will simply state they see more opportunities as an independent ongoing concern.

This contrasts with the idea of a friendly acquisition. In these more amicable types of corporate combinations, the two companies will be willing to mutually merge together. In a number of cases this will create a third company that is neither the buyer nor the target firm. It is more likely to occur in this manner when the two companies are similar in size.

Sometimes acquisitions start our friendly but turn into hostile takeovers quickly. A firm may demonstrate its clear interest in being purchased, or it may reject the idea either initially or after the fact. In these cases where they resist, the purchasing firm will be forced to aggressively buy huge stock share purchases in the target firm in order to gain a controlling majority. Only with a majority shareholder stake will such an acquisition actually occur under such circumstances.

How does a buying firm acquire such a controlling stake in a company that refuses to go along willingly with the hostile takeover in the first place? There are several ways in which they may proceed. The buying firm might propose a tender offer for present shareholders to sell them their stock share stakes. To persuade them to part with the shares, they would likely offer a significant premium over the then-current share price on the market. They would have to file a 30 day acquisition notice with the appropriate regulatory body the SEC Securities and Exchange Commission and also provide a copy to the target firm's hostile board of directors in order to complete such an offer.

In other cases, they might simply acquire shares of the target stock quietly on the open exchange, often through an intermediary brokerage partner. It is difficult to successfully obtain 51 percent of the stock this way though, as invariably the larger shareholders who may be institutional in nature will simply not be selling on the market, even as the price rises while the activity is taking place.

Companies can defend against hostile takeovers as well. Sometimes they are successful in this. There are a variety of defenses that have been effectively employed by target firms. The most potent of these are called poison pills. Companies can assume enormous amounts of corporate debt and then spend it in an effort to make the company more expensive and less attractive. The problem with this is that it can cause a firm serious financial repercussions later. Target companies have become bankrupt as a result of such actions, then liquidated and ultimately dissolved. There are unusual scenarios where companies elect to go bankrupt instead of being acquired. In such a defense called a Jonestown Defense, they deliberately take on so much debt that they become bankrupt.

A less extreme measure that is still a type of poison pill is called a Flip-in. This much more common variety of defenses against a hostile takeover permits present shareholders to purchase additional corporate treasury stock for a substantial discount when takeover offers occur. Such provisions are many times automatically triggered if a given single shareholder acquires anywhere in the 20 to 40 percent range of the common stock. The additional inexpensive shares dilutes the ownership pool of the company so that it is harder to acquire a majority controlling interest. It also decreases the value of the stake the prospective buying company has paid for already.

HSBC

HSBC stands for Hong Kong Shanghai Banking Corporation. This largest international bank in the world by balance sheet has over $1.63 trillion in total assets. The British London based banking giant counts more than 47 million customers as part of its international network spanning 71 countries and territories and 6,000 offices around the globe.

HSBC was founded by a British businessman in 1865 to finance the growing trade between the West and Asia, and especially China. Today HSBC remains among the largest and most impressive banking and financial services conglomerate groups in the world by any relevant measure. Their stated goal is to be recognized as the globe's foremost and best respected international bank.

HSBC is operated globally through four major divisions. These include its Commercial Banking, Global Banking and Markets, Private Banking, and Retail Banking and Wealth Management divisions. Among the banking group's many achievements over the centuries, the group was responsible for setting up the modern day Chinese currency and banking system back during the reign of the last Chinese imperial dynasty. This financial and currency system which HSBC established for China is still used today.

HSBC Commercial Banking operates throughout 55 different nations and territories. Their operation covers both developing and developed world markets that are most important to their many customers. The division serves a great variety of customer types, ranging from major multinational corporations to small outfits to medium sized companies. It offers them the financial tools they need to run their operations effectively.

One of the bank's most appealing features is that it can call upon its vast and multinational financial strength to support clients with term loans, project and acquisition finance, and daily working capital. The bank also offers its customers the financial and legal know how to assist them in engaging in effective stock and bond issues and offerings.

The commercial banking group supports specialist staff in four primary fields. Global Liquidity and Cash Management provides businesses with tools to effectively manage their liquidity. The online platform helps the customers to transact payments seamlessly between currencies and countries. Global Trade and Receivable Finance offers financing to suppliers and buyers in the trade cycle so that they can cover their supply chains.

Global Banking offers its commercial customers a variety of services such as capital financing via equity, debt, and advisory services. Insurance and Investments provides protection in the form of financial, business, and trade insurance. It also offers wealth management for corporations, employee benefits, and other commercial insurance products to protect against risk.

The Global Banking and Markets division works with customers to help them access commercial opportunities for developed and developing markets. This division operates in three groups including the corporate sector group, the resources and energy group, and the financial institutions group. Services and products are comprised of financing, advisory, research and analysis, prime services, trading and sales, securities services, and transaction banking.

HSBC Private Bank delivers global private banking services that include wealth management, investment, and private banking services to its individual, business, and executive clients. The division's goal is to become the world's foremost private bank for business owners who are high net worth individuals leveraging the group's longstanding globally leading commercial services and heritage.

Retail Banking and Wealth Management provides its tens of millions of customers with a broad range of products and services. These include personal banking, internet banking, loans, mortgages, savings, insurance, investments, and credit cards. They offer a variety of proprietary services and accounts that include HSBC Premier, HSBC Advance, personal online banking, financial planning, and wealth solutions.

Income Tax

Income tax refers to the tax on income which governments mandate for all personal and business entities and organizations which reside or are based in their jurisdiction. The law states that both individuals and businesses have to file their income tax returns once each year. Such filing demonstrates if they owe the government taxes or are instead able to claim a tax refund. This makes the tax on income a critical source of funding for governments. They employ it to pay for their various activities, goods, and services which they provide to the citizens and residents of their home country.

Income tax systems are usually progressive in nature. This is because national governments tend to understand that higher income earners have the broadest shoulders to bear the heaviest burdens of higher tax rates. The lower income earning individuals (and businesses) can not pay so much of their gross incomes.

The United States first imposed an income tax on its citizens in the time of the War of 1812. The goal for this tax was only to help repay the still-fledgling nation's $100 million worth of debt. They ran this up in the expenses related to the costly war on both land and sea. The government actually made good on its promise to repeal this tax on income after the conclusion of the war and repayment of the national war debt.

Despite this fact, income tax in America became a permanent fixture in the country in the early years of the twentieth century. The United States' entry into the First World War especially ran up enormous costs and debts for the nation. The tax never again disappeared in the U.S. The story is similar in many Western economically developed nations such as Great Britain, Canada, and others.

Within the U.S. today, it is the IRS Internal Revenue Service which carries the responsibility of enforcing tax laws and collecting these income taxes. They utilize a complicated and bureaucratic system of regulations and rules on incomes that have to be reported. They also monitor and decide which credits and deductions those filing individuals and businesses may claim. This agency collects the taxes from any type of income including wages, commissions, salaries, bonuses, investment earnings, and business income.

Individual income tax is one of the largest revenue generators for the Federal government of the United States today. The majority of citizens and residents within the country do not have to pay taxes on the entirety of their full earnings. Instead, the government utilizes a system of deductions on many different items to reduce the people's taxable income. Among these important deductions are dental and medical bills, interest on a mortgage, and educational expenses.

Taxpayers are allowed to minus these from their gross income in order to decide how much of their income is actually taxable. Should a taxpayer make $120,000 income and receive $20,000 worth of deductions, then the IRS will only impose taxes on the remainder of $100,000. After this, the tax agency will apply credits against the taxes which individuals owe. This means that an individual who owed $25,000 worth of taxes and received $5,000 in credits will only have to pay $20,000 total taxes.

Besides federal income taxes, a great number of the fifty states within the U.S. also collect their own state income taxes. Only seven states did not levy such taxes on their residents as of 2016. These lucky state residents lived in Wyoming, Washington state, Texas, South Dakota, Nevada, Florida, and Alaska. The two states of Tennessee and New Hampshire only levy such income taxes on any earnings realized from investments and dividends.

Businesses and corporations must also pay taxes on their earnings. The IRS deems any type of partnerships, corporations, small businesses, and even self-employed contractors to be businesses. Such groups must first report all of their business income and then subtract out their capital and operating expenses. What remains is called taxable business income.

Initial Public Offering (IPO)

An IPO is the acronym for an Initial Public Offering. Such IPO's represent the first opportunity for most investors to start buying shares of stock in the firm in question. Initial Public Offerings commonly generate a great deal of excitement, not only for the company involved but also for the members of the investing community.

Private companies decide to issue stock and become publicly traded companies for a few different reasons. The main two motivating factors revolve around the need to raise more capital, as well as the desire to permit the original business owners and investors to take profits on their time and investment that they originally put into starting up the company.

It is true that private companies are limited in the amount of capital that they are able to raise, since their ownership turns out to be restricted to certain organizations and individuals. Public companies have the advantages of allowing any investor to take a stake through buying stock shares on exchanges that are publicly traded. It is far easier for them to raise money as public companies.

Initial Public Offerings that go well translate to large amounts of cash for a company. They use this for future expansion and development. Those who began the company or who were initial investors typically make enormous gains at that time in compensation for their time and effort.

Initial Public Offerings take huge amounts of preliminary work. Great amounts of paper work have to be filled in and filed with the regulatory oversight groups. A prospectus has to be created for investors to study and consider. Advertising campaigns for the first shares that will be sold must be developed. On top of these tasks, the company has to continue its normal operations. Because of this, financial firms such as Morgan Stanley or Goldman Sachs are commonly engaged to perform these tasks on the company's behalf. Such a firm is called the IPO underwriting company. With enormous sized IPO's, these tasks could even be divided up between a few different IPO underwriting companies.

Contrary to what many people think, the majority of IPO's typically do not do well initially. Besides this, a percentage of the companies will not make it, meaning that all of the investment in the IPO stock could be lost. Because of this, there is great risk and often lower rewards for sinking money into Initial Public Offerings than in traditional well established companies and stocks. Many investors buy into the enthusiasm and excitement that surrounds Initial Public Offerings. Another explanation for their euphoria may have to do with believing that there is something special in being among the first investors to acquire the next possible Apple, Coca Cola, or IBM. Whatever their reasoning proves to be, investors continue to love Initial Public Offerings and the somewhat long shot opportunities that they represent.

Insolvency

Insolvency refers to the point where an individual, business, or even governmental organization is not able to cover its various financial obligations any longer. This means that it is unable to settle debts with its creditors and lenders as they are due. Many times, before such an indebted individual, company, or government becomes embroiled in any type of insolvency or bankruptcy procedures, they will try to enter into informal negotiations with creditors. This could involve setting up other payment schedules and arrangements.

Insolvency can happen for a variety of reasons. Among these is a decrease in cash flow and profitability forecasts, poor management of cash resources, or a rapid expansion in costs and expenses. Where businesses are concerned, this type of insolvency is classified according to one of two separate categories. The first of these is Cash Flow insolvency. This happens as a corporation or company simply can not pay the business debts as they become due. The second form is Balance Sheet insolvency. This type results from a company reaching the point where it possesses a negative net asset position. It simply means that the corporation's aggregate debts are greater than its total assets.

It is entirely possible for firms to be solvent by balance sheet figures but at the same time be insolvent by cash flow. The opposite scenario could also occur. If a company is bankrupt according to its balance sheet while still solvent by cash flow, it simply means its incoming revenues permit it to cover its current financial obligations. There are numerous companies which possess longer term debt obligations that continuously operate in this balance sheet-bankrupt status.

Technically, insolvency and bankruptcy are not exactly the same thing. The former is a condition of being in financial trouble or at least difficulties. Bankruptcy is instead a court order. It describes the ways in which a debtor which is no longer solvent will continue to meet its obligations or instead have its assets sold off to settle with the creditors.

This means that it is entirely possible for a company, individual, or government entity to be no longer solvent but not yet be officially bankrupt. This could result from a temporary or sometimes fixable problem. The reverse is never the case. An entity can not be bankrupt yet still be solvent. Such a lack of solvency often translates into an eventual bankrupt state when the debtors are not able to improve their financial conditions.

Corporations and firms that have become insolvent are able to improve their financial state. They might slash costs, borrow money, sell their assets, renegotiate the terms of their debts, or seek out a bigger corporation to acquire them. The buyer could settle their debts as part of the assumption of their services, products, technology, and proprietary trademarks.

Several unfortunate events can lead to a company becoming insolvent. If they do not have enough management in human resources or accounting departments, this could contribute to the problem. A lack of qualified accounting staff could cause a company's budget to be either ignored or misappropriated.

There might also be sharply increasing vendor prices which the company is powerless to stop. Higher prices for their goods and services mean that companies will have to raise their prices in an effort to pass these along to the consumer. The problem arises when customers then shop another company or product to get a better price. Lost clientele nearly always translates into a drop in cash flow. This means that they no longer have the cash coming in to cover the bills due to the company creditors.

There could also be lawsuits brought by employees or customers that break a company's finances. The firm could be forced to pay enormous bills for both defense and in settlement damages which make it impossible for them to continue ongoing operations. As operations cease and revenue naturally drops, the ability to pay bills disappears quickly.

A final reason centers on the lack of evolution in a company product line. It might be customers simply change their needs and therefore purchasing habits. This could lead them to rival firms which offer a broader product range or line. The company which could not or did not adapt its products will find its revenues and profits decreasing to the point where they are unable to cover their expenses with their remaining income.

Intangible Assets

Intangible assets refer to the possessions of a company that are not physical. They are difficult to quantify for several reasons. These types of assets can not be physically measured. They also represent an unknown or undetermined cash value to a company. Several criteria for intangible assets are that they are invisible and can not be touched. Despite this interesting characteristic they are intrinsically valuable. These assets prove to be critical to the overall success of any business.

Intangible assets are typically classed in two categories. These are legal assets and competitive assets. Legal assets are easier to understand than are competitive assets. Legal assets include the wide varieties of intellectual and creative property. In this category are such important holdings as patents, copyrights, brand names, trade secrets, and trademarks.

Each of these can be owned and has value, though it is not easy to assign a value to these elements. Patents are the rights to inventions. Copyrights give ownership of writings and similar creative property. Brand names are a company's physical name or product, such as Coca Cola, McDonald's, or Big Mac.

Trade secrets refer to a company's ways of making things that are not known to rivals and competitors. The formula for Coca Cola is a well-known example of a trade secret. Trademarks are the ownership of popular company or product slogans or phrases as used in advertising.

The second category of intangible assets is the competitive intangible assets. These are more abstract and difficult to grasp. Competitive assets refer to reputation and the knowledge of how to do things for the business. Such assets as these can be obtained with experience mostly. These types of assets include human capital, know how, leveraging, reputation, and collaboration. Naming such ideas is hard enough, but assigning them values is a matter of conjecture.

There are reasons why coming up with values on such intangible assets is so incredibly hard. Valuing properties means that an analyst must gaze into a company's future to determine the ways that these assets will impact its bottom line in the coming years. In the process they take the assets' cost and allocate it through the expected life of the asset. Some intangible assets are valued in legal terms. An intangible asset will never be given a longer life span than forty years. When the analysts and accountants do this allocation, it is referred to as amortizing the intangible assets.

Another division of intangible assets is the category of either definite or indefinite assets. With definite assets, individuals are referring to those that will endure for a specific amount of time. Contract agreements are good examples of these types.

Indefinite assets can last for an indefinite time span. A well-known example of this is a company's brand name. Such an asset will endure so long as the enterprise keeps making the products.

Intangible assets may be hard to value, but they are still valuable for a company. Clearly an intangible asset can not have the same easily assessable value that a physical plant or other equipment would. Such intangible assets are often of great value to the company though.

There are many cases of such a property being instrumental in the company's eventual success or failure. McDonald's is so wildly successful because of the tremendous value it gains from consumer recognition of its brand name. This recognition can not be physically touched or seen.

The results of its impact on the company profits are unquestionably valuable to McDonald's. The strength of their global brand pushes sales around the world on every year. These intangible assets like brands are so powerful precisely because they make an impact on customers' choices. This allows companies to charge higher prices for their products.

Interest Rate

Interest rates are the levels at which interest is charged a borrower for using money that they obtain in the form of a loan from a bank or other lender. These are also the rates that individuals and businesses are paid for depositing their funds with a bank. Interest rates are central to the running of capitalist economies. They are commonly written out as percentage rates for a given time frame, most commonly per year.

As an example, a small business might require capital to purchase new assets for the company. To acquire these, they borrow money form a bank. In exchange for making them this loan, the bank is paid interest at a pre set and agreed upon rate of interest for lending it to the company and putting off their own use of the monies. They receive this interest in monthly payments along with repayments of the principal.

Interest rates are also used by government agencies in pursuing monetary policies. Central banks set them to influence their nation's economic performance. They impact many elements of an economy such as unemployment, inflation, and investment levels.

There are several different interest rates to consider. The most commonly expressed one is the nominal interest rate. This nominal interest rate proves to be the amount of interest that is payable in money terms. If a family deposits $1,000 in a bank for a year, and is paid $50 in interest, then their balance by the conclusion of the year will be $1,050. This would translate to a nominal interest rate amounting to five percent per year.

The real interest rate is another type of rate used to determine how much purchasing power is received. It is the interest rate after the level of inflation is subtracted. Determining the real interest rate is a matter of calculating the nominal rate and removing the amount of inflation from it. In the example above, supposed the economy's inflation level is measured at five percent for the year. This would mean that the $1,050 in the account at year end only buys what it did as $1,000 at the beginning of the year. This translates to a real interest rate of zero.

Interest rates change for many reasons. They are altered for political gains of parties in power. By reducing the interest rate, an economy gains a short term boost. The help to the economy will often influence the outcome of elections. Unfortunately, the short term advantage gained is often offset later by inflation. This reason for changing interest rates is eliminated with independent central banks.

Another main reason that interest rates change is because of expectations of inflation. Since the majority of economies demonstrate inflation, fixed amounts of money will purchase fewer goods a year from now than they will today. Lenders expect to be compensated for this. Central banks raise interest rates to fight this inflation as necessary.

Interim Financing

Interim financing is a way of obtaining funding on a short term basis for a project. It can also be called gap financing or bridge financing. People or companies elects for this kind of financing for a specific purpose.

They may be seeking to get funding so that a project can be finished and start creating revenues. This would keep them from having to take resources away from other projects. This concept generally refers to loans. There are also cases of interim financing where companies utilize grants or other types of financial assistance.

A short term loan proves to be among the most frequently employed types of interim financing. These kinds of loans can be crafted so that the borrower will pay back the entire principle of the loan along with all of its interest in twelve months or less from the loan issue date.

This is the opposite of long term financing. In the longer term variety, the borrower receives several years to repay the loan. Loan deals on gap financing often come with interest rates that are a little higher than with longer term loans. For individuals or companies with excellent credit, financing companies can often offer extremely competitive interest rates on these short term loans.

A common use of interim financing is with construction projects that need to be finished. On an individual level, a consumer may wish to renovate either a room in the house or the entire home. The borrower may decide to obtain a short term loan at a better interest rate to cover the costs of labor and materials at the beginning of the project. This can save the borrower on the more substantial interest rates and fees for using credit cards or store credit with the various vendors. The end result is that the consumer spends significantly less money on the improvement project than he or she would by not utilizing the interim financing.

Real estate deals are another common use for this interim financing. A home owner may wish to move forward and buy a new house. The owner may need their present house to sell first. Short term loans like these can prove to be an optimal answer to the problem. Using the bridge loan the owner buys the house. The borrower can then repay the loan once their original house sells. This kind of strategy will help to push through the sale of the original house as well. The previous owners have already moved, which means the new owners can occupy the property without delay.

The goal of interim financing is to offer a short term bridge loan for the individual or business concerned. Despite this, sometimes a situation develops where the borrower will not be able to repay the loan as quickly as hoped. In this case, longer term or additional financing becomes necessary. Many lenders will work with the borrower in such a case to come up with a longer term financing program.

This will completely pay off the short term original loan. Additional money will usually be provided so that the borrower has the funds necessary to complete the project. This is especially the case with construction companies. It works out better for the borrower to engage in a rollover longer term loan than to take out another short term loan. The reason for this is that the longer term loans' finance rates are nearly always lower than the most competitive rates lenders will offer borrowers for short term bridge loans.

Internal Rate of Return (IRR)

The IRR is the acronym for internal rate of return. This IRR proves to be the capital budget rate of return that is utilized in order to determine and compare and contrast various investments' profitability. It is sometimes known as the discounted cash flow rate of return alternatively, or even the ROR, or rate of return. Where banks are concerned, the IRR is also known as the effective interest rate. The word internal is used to specify that such calculation does not involve facts that are part of the external environment, such as inflation or the interest rate.

More precisely, the internal rate of return for any investment proves to be the interest rate level where the negative cash flow, or net present value of costs, from the investment is equal to the positive cash flow, or net present value of benefits, for the investment. In other words, this IRR will yield a discount rate that causes the net current values of both positive and negative cash flows of a specific investment to cancel out at zero.

These Internal Rates of Return are generally utilized to consider projects and investments and their ultimate desirability. Naturally, a project will be more appealing to engage in or purchase if it comes with a greater internal rate of return. Given a number of projects from which to choose, and assuming that all project benefits prove to be the same generally, the project that contains the greatest Internal Rate of Return will be considered the most attractive. It should be selected with the highest priority of being pursued first.

The assumed theory for companies is that they will be interested in eventually pursuing any investment or project that comes with an IRR that is greater than the expense of the money put into the project as capital. The number of projects or investments that can be run at a time are limited in the real world though. A firm may have a restricted capability of overseeing a large number of projects at once, or they may lack the necessary funds to engage in all of them at a time.

The internal rate of return is actually a number expressed as a percent. It details the yield, efficacy, and efficiency of a given investment or project. This should not be confused with the net present value that instead tells the particular investment's actual value.

In general, a given investment or project is deemed to be worthwhile assuming that its internal rate of return proves to be higher than either the expense of the capital involved, or alternatively, than a pre set minimally accepted rate of return. For companies that possess share holders, the minimum IRR is always a factor of the investment capital's cost. This is easily decided by ascertaining the cost of capital, which is risk adjusted, for alternative types of investments. In this way, share holders will approve of a project or investment, so long as its Internal Rate of Return is greater than the cost of the capital to be used and this project or investment creates economic value that is viable for the company in question.

Joint Venture

Joint ventures are businesses or projects that two or more companies create together. They typically have shared risks and returns, ownership, and control structure. Companies form joint ventures for a primary reason. Usually they are trying to combine their various resources in order to achieve some specific goal. It could be for an existing or a new project. Each of the JV owners is ultimately liable for the losses, profits, and costs that come with it. The joint venture itself is a separate company that has different objectives from the main interests of the owning companies.

Companies form joint ventures as a means to pool their expertise in the industry, their business reputation, their technology and abilities, and their separate human resources. This gives them the advantage of combining resources on a project as they are able to share the costs, liabilities, and risks associated with the job.

Joint ventures are most often temporary partnerships between two or more companies. They draw up contracts that spell out the joint project terms for which every participant will be responsible. At the end of the joint venture, every participating party gets its shared percentage of the losses or profits. They sign an agreement that the joint venture is over and dissolve the original JV agreement. These are among the advantages for forming such joint ventures.

There are many disadvantages to these joint ventures as well. Because of these, as many as half of the JVs ever formed end with conflict in under four years' time. Among the problems that plague joint ventures are greater liability, reduced outside opportunities, and unfair divisions of resources and work.

Greater liability is a serious and real issue for the owners of joint ventures. Most joint ventures become set up with structures of limited liability companies or partnerships. Each of these types of business structure comes with its own liability. Only if they form a business entity that is separate can they avoid this increased liability for the JV. All participating owners equally share responsibility for any claims that are filed against the JV. This is true regardless of how much they are involved in the activity that instigated the claims.

Contracts with joint ventures also typically reduce the amount of outside opportunities for all of the companies participating. This lasts so long as the joint venture project is ongoing. There are often non-compete agreements and exclusivity arrangements made in the process. These agreements will impact their business dealings with vendors and customers alike. The idea is to keep all parties focused on the joint venture's success and to reduce conflicts of interest between their various businesses. These limitations will end after the project concludes. In the meantime, they can negatively affect the main business and operations of the various partner companies.

Unfair divisions of resources and work are a final problem that haunts many joint ventures. The parties involved all share control and ownership. This does not mean that the employment of resources and amount of work done will be fairly divided. One company might only have to put people to work on the project while another has to provide facilities, technology, or access to distribution. This may mean a lot more work and resources are committed by the one partner.

Despite this unfair burden, the shares of the profits are the same for all contributors. It does not matter that one partner often contributes much more to the project. Such unfair distributions of work and resources often cause conflicts among the owners of the JV project. Conflicts like this can create a lower rate of success for the project in the end.

JP Morgan Chase

JP Morgan Chase turns out to be among the oldest financial institutions or banks that are based in the United States. The firm's history hails back more than 200 years. Today, the company boasts assets that exceed $2.4 trillion, and it is a leading global banking and financial services outfit. JP Morgan Chase has a presence in over 100 countries and maintains more than 235,000 employees around the globe in over 450 corporate offices.

JP Morgan Chase counts millions of individuals and small businesses as customers of the banking group. They serve some of the most important governments, institutions, and corporations in the world. JP Morgan proves to be one of the global leaders in financial services for individuals and small businesses, investment banking, commercial banking, asset management, and financial transactions and processing. One of their proudest achievements as a testament to their importance in the United States is the fact that their company stock is one of the only 30 company components of the famed Dow Jones Industrial Average.

JP Morgan Chase & Company proves to be not only one of the oldest and biggest financial institutions in the world, but also among the best known such organizations on earth. The earliest predecessor of the banking group received its charter in New York City in 1799. The company has an aggressive history of mergers and acquisitions that have seen over 1,200 predecessor banking and financial institutions merged into the present day form of the banking behemoth.

Among its most important legacy firms are J.P. Morgan, Chase Manhattan Bank, Chemical Bank, and Manufacturers Hanover of New York City as well as Bank One, National Bank of Detroit, and First Chicago in the Midwest. These institutions each held important ties for their day and age to progress in finance and the expansion of both the American and world economies.

The mega mergers of the banking group began in 2000 when J.P. Morgan & Co. Inc. merged together with the Chase Manhattan Corporation. In this merger, J.P. Morgan, Chase, Manufacturers Hanover, and Chemical became one enormous financial conglomerate. This at last combined four of the biggest, most important, and oldest banking center groups of New

York City together under the single entity name and ownership of J.P. Morgan Chase & Co.

The activity continued in 2004. J.P. Morgan Chase & Company merged with Chicago's Bank One Corporation. At the time, the New York Times newspaper claimed that the combination would remake the competitive landscape of banking as it tied together the commercial and investment banking prowess of J.P. Morgan Chase with the significant consumer banking abilities of the Midwestern-based Bank One.

In 2008, JP Morgan Chase acquired the world's largest savings and loan Washington Mutual Bank as a result of the biggest bank failure in history. Gaining control of Washington Mutual's substantial banking operations meant that the banking group expanded its consumer branches into Florida, California, and Washington State for the first time. This formed the second biggest network of bank locations in the United States whose branches reached an astonishing 42% of all people living in the U.S.

That same year in the depths of the financial crisis, JP Morgan Chase took over the collapsing Wall Street firm The Bear Stearns Companies. This improved the group's swelling abilities in a wide variety of businesses such as global energy trading, cash clearing, and prime brokerage. The group rounded out its presence in the United Kingdom in 2010 by gaining full ownership of its original British joint venture J.P. Morgan Cazenove. This joint venture was among the most premier investment banks in Britain.

Junk Bonds

Junk bonds are almost the same as regular bonds with an important difference. They are lower rated for credit worthiness. This is why in order to understand junk bonds, individuals first must comprehend the basics of traditional bonds.

Like traditional bonds, junk bonds are promises from organizations or companies to pay back the holder the amount of money which they borrow. This amount is known as the principal. Terms of such bonds involve several elements. The maturity date is the time when the borrower will repay the bond holder. There will also be an interest rate that the bond holder receives, or a coupon. Junk bonds are unlike those traditional ones because the credit quality of the issuing organization is lower.

Every kind of bond is rated according to its credit quality. Bonds can all be categorized in one of two types. Investment grade bonds possess medium to low risk. Their credit ratings are commonly in the range of from AAA to BBB. The downside to these bonds is that they do not provide much in the way of interest returns. Their advantage is that they have significantly lower chances of the borrower being unable to make interest payments.

Junk bonds on the other hand offer higher interest yields to their bond holders. Issuers do this because they do not have any other way to finance their needs. With a lower credit rating, they can not borrow capital at a more favorable price. The ratings on such junk bonds are often BB or less from Standard & Poor's or Ba or less by Moody's rating agency. Bond ratings such as these can be considered like a report card for the credit rating of the company in question. Riskier firms receive lower ratings while safe blue-chip companies earn higher ratings.

Junk bonds typically pay an average yield that is from 4% to 6% higher than U.S. Treasury yields. These types of bonds are placed into one of two categories. These are fallen angels and rising stars. Fallen angels bonds used to be considered at an investment grade. They were cut to junk bond level as the company that issued them saw its credit quality decline.

Rising stars are the opposites of fallen angels. This means the rating of the bond has risen. As the underlying issuer's credit quality improves, so does the rating of the bond. Rising stars are often still considered to be junk bonds. They are on track to rise to investment quality.

Junk bonds are risky for more reasons than the chances of not receiving one or more interest payments. There is the possibility of not receiving the original principal back. This type of investing also needs a great amount of skills in analyzing data like special credit. Because of these risk factors and specialized skills that are needed, institutional investors massively dominate the market.

A better way for individuals to become involved with junk bonds is through high yield bond funds. Professionals research and manage the holdings of these funds. The risks associated with a single bond defaulting are greatly reduced. They do this by diversifying into a variety of companies and types of bonds. High yield bond funds often require investors to stay invested for minimally a year or two.

When the yield of junk bonds declines below the typical 4% to 6% spread above Treasuries, investors should be careful. The risk does not become less in these cases. It is that the returns no longer justify the dangers in the junk bonds. Investors also should carefully consider the junk bond default rates. These can be tracked for free on Moody's website.

Levied Taxes

Levied taxes are taxes that are forcefully collected from an individual, business, or other entity. Among the many taxes most frequently collected these days are income taxes. These taxes could be said to be levied, since the law requires that an individual's income tax is levied for the government by the company where they work.

Three main types of tax systems are in effect in the world today where income is concerned. These include progressive, proportional, and regressive tax systems. Progressive taxes levied are those that employ progressively greater rates of tax as earnings are higher. As an example, the first $10,000 that an individual makes might be taxed at only five percent, while the next $10,000 is possibly taxed at a rate of ten percent, and income above this could be taxed at a twenty percent rate.

Proportional taxes use a pre set flat rate of tax. This applies to all earnings, no matter how high or low they are. With a ten percent flat rate, everyone will pay their ten percent of income as taxes levied, regardless of what amount of money they actually make.

Regressive taxes are said to hurt the poor by shifting the tax burden to lower income earners. This type of tax levy only taxes income to a certain dollar level, such as the first $80,000. Any money made above this amount would simply not be taxed. In reality, most tax systems employ the various kinds of tax levying methods to address various forms of income.

Levied taxes also apply to corporations and businesses. The income of a company is taxed in what is known as a corporate tax. This is sometimes alternatively referred to as a profit tax or corporate income tax. With corporate taxes levied, the net income is generally the figure that is taxed. Net income refers to the difference of gross income and expenses and other allowable write offs.

With individuals, the total income for a family or individual is commonly taxed. Some deductions are usually allowed before the taxes to be levied are determined. Income may be reduced by a certain amount as a result of how many children a family has to support, as an example.

There are many other forms of taxes levied in modern capitalist countries such as Great Britain and the United States. More than two hundred different types of taxes can be identified in the U.S. alone. These include such various taxes levied as income tax, sales tax, property tax, estate tax, capital gains tax, dividends tax, gasoline taxes, leisure taxes, luxury items taxes, and so called sin taxes on items such as cigarettes and alcohol. The United States has been called the most heavily taxed society in all of world history.

Liabilities

Where a business is concerned, liabilities prove to be amounts of money that are owed by the company at any given point. These liabilities are displayed on the firm's balance sheet. They are commonly listed as items payable, or simply as payables.

There are two types of liabilities. These are longer term liabilities and shorter term liabilities. Long term liabilities turn out to be business obligations that last for greater than the period of a single year. Mortgages payable and loans payable are included in this category.

Short term liabilities represent business obligations that will be paid in less than a year. There are many different kinds of short term liabilities. They include all of the items detailed below.

Payroll taxes payable are one of these. They represent sums automatically collected from the employees and put to the side by the employer. They have to be given to the IRS and any state taxing agencies at the pre determined time.

Sales taxes payable are another short term liability. The business collects them from its customers when sales are made. They hold them until it is time to give them to the proper revenue collecting department within the state.

Mortgages and loans payable are another short term liability. These represent payments made every month on mortgages and loans. They are not large single payments or the total amount of a loan that is eventually owed, but instead represent recurring monthly obligations.

Liabilities for individuals are another type of liabilities altogether. They also represent money that has to be paid out. For people, they are debts owed, as well as monthly cash flow that goes out of the individual's accounts.

Liabilities and assets are the opposites of each other, yet people often get them confused. While assets are things that contribute positive cash flow to a person's finances, liabilities are those that create negative cash flow, or money that leaves an individual's accounts every month. For example, a house that an individual owes money on and makes monthly payments on is a liability, not an asset. The house takes money from the person in the form of monthly mortgage payments each month. For a house to be an asset, it would have to be completely paid off. Even still, if monthly taxes and insurance payments are being made, then technically it would still be a liability. Houses can only be assets really and truly when they are rented out and the rental income that a person receives is greater than all of the expenses associated with the house every month, including any mortgage payments, taxes, insurance, upkeep, and property management fees. When the net result of a property is money coming in, then it is an asset and not a liability.

Liquidation

The meaning of liquidation depends on the use of the word. In financial terms, there are three different definitions of it. In economics or finance it refers to a failed company. A company that is insolvent is unable to pay its bills when they are owed. Liquidation is the process of winding up the company. The operations of the company cease at this point. The assets would then be divided up among its creditors and stock holders. This is done based on whose claims have priority.

Insolvent companies that choose to go into liquidation generally do so under U.S. bankruptcy code Chapter 7. This legal statute gives the rules on liquidation of companies. Companies that are still solvent but are in trouble may also file a Chapter 7 bankruptcy. This is less common. There are also bankruptcies for companies that do not force liquidation. One such provision that covers this scenario is Chapter 11. In a Chapter 11 filing the trustee saves the company and restructures its debts.

When the process of liquidation occurs, the company halts all operations. All of its assets are tallied up and then distributed to the various claimants. After this is finished, the trustee finally dissolves the business. The debts actually have not been discharged in this process. They still exist to the point where the statute of limitations on the debts expires. There is no debtor in existence to pay off these debts. Creditors simply write them off in practice.

The assets in this liquidation process are handled in a certain methodical way. The Department of Justice appoints a trustee. This individual supervises the process. Assets are distributed to those who have claims based on their priority. Secured creditors are first in line. This is because their loans are backed up by collateral.

The lenders are allowed to seize this collateral and then to sell it. Many times they receive far less than the actual asset value because there are limited time frames. Sometimes the assets are not enough to cover their debt. These creditors are compensated from any other liquid assets in this case.

Unsecured creditors come next in the process. In this category are holders of bonds, the IRS, and employees. Bond holders are a form of unsecured creditors. The company may owe the IRS taxes. Employees may be waiting on payroll or other money they are due. The last category to receive compensation is shareholders. If any assets are left they receive them. Preferred stock investors receive priority before the common stock holders. Usually there is nothing left for either class by the time the creditors are paid.

Another definition of liquidation surrounds huge sales. Sometimes a company needs to close out a great deal of inventory. They would do this by liquidating their inventory at deep discounts. Any company can do this. They do not have to file for bankruptcy in order to sell off inventory.

A third definition of liquidation involves closing out an investment. This generally occurs when an investors sells their holdings in exchange for cash. An individual might also liquidate out of a one position and into an opposite one. If he or she held long shares in a stock, they could instead take on the identical number of short shares.

Brokers can force liquidate trader positions in certain cases. Traders who have acted or traded recklessly with risk can have this happen. If traders' account values drop below the minimum margin requirements they can suffer from forced liquidation as well.

Liquidation Value

Liquidation Value represents the full value of a corporation's complete range of physical assets if and when it declares bankruptcy or actually goes out of business. This value is compiled when every asset on the company books and balance sheet becomes tallied up. This value then includes real estate, equipment, factories, fixtures, and inventory. Those assets that are intangible would never be a part of the firm's final liquidating value.

This is one of four key types of value assigned to a corporation or company's various assets. These include book value, market value, salvage value, and liquidation value. With every category of value, this delivers an alternative view point for both analysts and accountants alike to classify the total value of all assets. For individuals and investors who engage in workouts and bankruptcies, this Liquidating Value is absolutely essential to know.

Book value and market value generally vie for the crown of largest assets' category valuation. In cases where any group of assets' market value has deteriorated because of decreasing market demand instead of the business using it up, this proves to be true. With book value, the asset value equates to the one declared upon the corporate balance sheet. Since the company balance sheet declares these assets for their historical price and cost, this means that the book value could equate to more or less than the relevant market prices which apply on a given day. When the all around economy is growing and prices in general are rising, then this book value is traditionally less than the relevant market value.

With liquidation value, the sum represents the anticipated price for the asset after it has been sold, generally for a loss as compared the original price. Salvage value refers to the one assigned to the assets once they reach the conclusion of their natural and useful life. This then would represent the scrap value of assets. Liquidation value typically proves to be less than the book and market values yet still higher than basic salvage value. Liquidating assets are still valuable, they just sell for less than they otherwise should and would because of the proverbial fire sale in a shortened time frame. It causes them to be sold for losses versus their listed book value.

There are reasons why such liquidation values never include any intangible asset prices. Such intangible assets comprise the goodwill, intellectual property, and brand recognition of the company or corporation. When firms are sold off instead of being liquidated, the firm's value will include both intangible assets' value and liquidation value. This is why traditional value investors will consider and contemplate the variances between the ongoing concern value and the market cap value. They are able to decide this way whether or not the stock of the corporation represents a good value.

It is always useful to consider an example in order to clarify the concept of liquidation value. A given corporation the Snappy Pop Company has $550,000 in liabilities. They also possess book valued assets of $1 million on their company balance sheet. The auction value of these assets might be $750,000, which represents three-quarters of their fair value. At the same time, the salvage value is $75,000. To determine the liquidation value, analysts simply subtract out any liabilities (in this case $550,000) off of the auction value (in this case $750,000). This gives a value of $750,000 minus $550,000 for a grand total of $200,000 liquidating value.

Loan Syndication

Loan Syndication refers to the procedure of getting a few different lenders involved in delivering a few different components of a loan. This activity typically happens in those situations where borrowers need to borrow a huge amount of capital. In these cases, the money required might be more than any one lender will feel comfortable providing or could be higher than certain lenders' levels of allowed risk exposure. This is why many lenders choose to work hand in glove on such projects in order to deliver the financing a borrower requires.

Corporate borrowing typically involves this type of loan syndication such firms look for loans to cover a wide range of needs. It is most often needed as companies are attempting to perform an acquisition, a merger, or a share buyback, or for other kinds of capital intensive projects. With a capital project of this nature, significant loans will be involved. This is why these loan syndications are utilized for these types of projects or merger and acquisition activity.

This kind of Loan Syndication permits any single lender to be involved with more than only a single huge loan. It also allows it to keep a more manageable and sensible level of credit exposure since it is not the one creditor involved with the deal in question. In these types of multi bank underwritten deals, the various lenders' terms will commonly be identical to the borrower, although there are incidents where this is not the case and they instead vary. The various lenders will often require different amounts of collateral. These requirements can vary significantly. It is common however for there to almost always be a single loan agreement which governs the whole of the syndicate group.

With the majority of Loan Syndication, one financial institution plays the role of lead bank. They will then arrange all terms and particulars of the deal itself. This lead financial institution is commonly referred to as the deal's syndicate agent. Such an agent is commonly responsible to handle all particulars of the deal. This means they will arrange the upfront transaction, compliance reports, fees, loan monitoring, reporting, and repayment arrangements in the life of the loan. They do this on behalf of every lender who is a party to the deal.

There can be specialists brought in to help with some aspects of the deal in question. These are typically third parties which are not a part of the loan syndicate. They often handle such important administrative functions as monitoring and report making. With loan syndications, there are many times higher fees to cover the huge reporting requirements as well as to finalize, package up, and handle the loan servicing and processing. This means that fees can run up to 10 percent of the principal of the loan amount.

For the year 2015, the company with the greatest amount of loan funded syndications on its books was Charter Communications. They boasted of $13.8 billion in syndicate amounts thanks to the merger transaction with Time Warner Cable. The lead financial institution on the syndication was Credit Suisse. For the loan market of the United States, the banks which represent the foremost lead institutions with loan syndications prove to be Bank of America Merrill Lynch, Wells Fargo, JPMorgan, and Citi.

There is an umbrella organization which covers the corporate loan market. This is the LSTA Loan Syndications and Trading Association. There goals are to offer resources for those firms interested in participating in loan syndications as well as those companies that require the services of loans in this capacity. It brings together all of the various important players in the market, delivers market research on relevant topics, and even lobbies industry regulators to impact procedures for compliance in Washington, London, and other important loan syndication cities around the world.

Loan to Cost Ratio

Loan to Cost Ratio, or LTC, proves to be a measurement utilized by finance companies in extending loans for commercial real estate projects. It is employed ultimately to make comparisons of the offered financing for a given building project versus the expenses of completing said project. With the LTC ratio, lenders of commercial real estate loans are able to decide on the risks involved in backing a particular construction project via loans. The LTC ratio is similar to the LTV loan to value ratio. They both compare the amount of the construction loan to the value in fair market terms of the project in question.

Lenders work with the Loan to Cost Ratio in order to decide what loan percentage or dollar amount the financier is agreeable to finance. They do this with a basis on the firm costs stated in the construction project budget. After construction completes, these projects then possess a new and often times significantly higher value. Future values can often be double what the construction costs prove to be. This means that on a loan for $200,000 in construction, the future value of the project is likely to be $400,000 once it is fully concluded.

Consider how LTC will look in this example. With $200,000 in construction costs, and an 80% LTC ratio, the lender would be willing to loan out $160,000 on the total project. Using a similar 80% LTV ratio metric instead would significantly change the amount of money the lender is wiling to extend to $400,000 x 80% for $320,000.

Lenders never completely finance 100% of construction costs. This is because they feel that the builders also need to have significant exposure to the project in order to guarantee they will give their all to see them succeed. This is what is meant by the colloquial expression "skin in the game." It prevents a builder from simply getting up and walking away from a project gone bad. It is why the majority of lenders will require a builder to kick in minimally 10% to 20% of the construction costs to secure a financing deal.

Loan to value ratios are not the same as the Loan to Cost Ratio, though they have much in common up to a point. LTV evaluates the loan issued versus the project value once it will be fully completed. Since most banks assume that construction projects will double in value once they are finished, this is why an identical LTV percentage to the LTC ratio will yield twice the loan amount.

Lenders hold firmly to the LTC ratio. It helps them to clearly express the levels of risk in a given financing project for commercial construction. In the end, using a greater Loan to Cost Ratio will entail a significantly riskier project from the lender's perspective. This is why the overwhelming majority of reputable mainstream lenders will not surpass a pre-determined percentage when they consider any given project. They usually limit this amount strictly to a maximum of 80% of the project's LTV or LTC. When lenders are willing to become involved at a higher percentage and ratio, they will most always insist on a substantially greater project and loan interest rate to compensate them for the additional level of risk to which they are consenting.

Lenders will also have to consider other information and circumstances beyond simply Loan to Cost Ratio and Loan to value ratios when extending such financing. They take into consideration the value of the property and its location for where the project will be constructed. They also contemplate how much creditworthiness and experience the commercial builders in the application possess. Finally, they consult both the borrowers' loan payment histories on other loans and their credit record as demonstrated in their company credit report.

Margin

Margin refers to a term used by companies and corporations in business. It is the spread between the firm's product or service sales price and the cost to make it. Another way of putting this is the ratio of firm's revenue to expenses. Margin can be utilized to refer to profit margins, operating margins, net margins, pretax profit margins, and gross profit margins.

Profit margin is the larger catch all category for many of these margins. Analysts and businesses figure it as the total net income divided by the firm's revenues. Another way of deriving it is through net profits divided by sales. Coming up with the net income is not hard. It requires that individuals subtract out the total of a firm's given expenses. This means that all material costs, operating costs, interest expenses, and taxes costs will have to be deducted from the total revenue. Such profit margins become expressed in percentage terms. In practice they measure the amount from each dollar in sales that the corporation gets to keep as earnings.

The other business margins are not difficult to understand and are simply variations on profit margins. With gross profit margins, the phrase displays the connection between firms' total sales revenues and their COGS cost of goods sold. Conversely, operating profit margins consider the cost of goods sold along with the operating expenses. They compare these against the revenues. Finally, net profit margins gather all of these expenses, interest paid on loans and bonds, and taxes to compare them to total sales revenues.

It is always useful to look at practical examples to better understand complex concepts. Consider a company like Burger King. They might claim an 18 percent profit margin. This would mean that after they paid their expenses, labor costs, material costs, any interest on debt, and taxes, they would have left 18 cents on every dollar of sales revenues they realized. Margin can have several other meanings as well.

A common one has to do with investor accounts. Many stock or options' account holders will have what industry personnel call a margin account. This permits the investors to be able to purchase their securities on margin. They may buy a stock or option by only having to pay a certain set and predetermined percentage of the cost of the investment. The remaining cost they simply borrow from the brokerage firm or the associated bank of the firm.

In most cases, the broker becomes the lender and carries out these functions as expected. This means that they enforce the collateral requirement and minimum maintenance requirements. The securities which the investor purchased using the margin account become the collateral for the balance of the loan. This will commonly be expressed using a percentage.

Consider an example of this to better understand the idea. Investors may purchase $10,000 in stocks with margin. As the rate is set by the brokerage firm at 25 percent, they will have to deposit and pay $2,500 of their own cash. The remainder $7,500 they simply borrow from the brokerage company (or bank). This makes great sense for those investors who predict that the return they will realize on the investments will significantly outweigh the cost of the loans.

Margins are also utilized as a concept with regards to mortgages. Some particular mortgages are called ARMs, or adjustable rate mortgages. They provide a fixed interest rate during some type of introductory time frame. At that point, the rate adjusts up (sometimes dramatically). Banks figure up this new rate by simply adding margins on to the pre-established index. Such margins typically remain fixed during the remainder of the loan's life span. Yet the rate of the index can and will change.

Market Capitalization

Market capitalization refers to a company's total value. Analysts determine it by multiplying the number of shares in existence times the price of the stock. This concept can also be utilized to measure the full value of a stock exchange. The New York Stock Exchange market capitalization would equal the value of all publicly traded companies on the exchange added together.

Market cap is another name for market capitalization. Examples of how this is figured make it easier to understand. Companies that have 2 million shares which have been issued that sell for $20 apiece have a market cap of $40 million. If an investor had enough money and could get the stockholders to agree to sell their shares, he or she could purchase the company for $40 million total. In practice many shareholders would want more than the current share price to sell their stock.

There are three different main sizes of market capitalization among traded companies. These are large cap, mid cap, and small cap corporations. Large cap companies are generally considered the least risky ones in which to invest. They typically possess substantial financial resources to survive economic downturns. They are also generally leaders in their industries. This gives them a smaller amount of growth opportunity.

Because of this the returns for these large cap companies are often not as spectacular as with successful companies in the other two categories. They also have a significantly greater chance of paying dividends out to their share holders. Large cap corporations have $5 billion and higher capitalization.

Mid cap companies are generally less risky than the smaller companies. They still do not have the same possibilities for aggressive growth. Mid cap companies commonly possess market capitalization of from $1 billion to $5 billion. Studies have shown that mid caps have outperformed large cap and small cap corporation stocks in the past 20 years.

Small cap corporations are those which possess under $1 billion in market capitalization. These tinier companies have often completed an Initial Public Offering in the recent past. Such companies are considered the riskiest of the three types. This is because in economic downturns, they have the greatest chance of failing or defaulting. They also enjoy plenty of opportunity and space to expand. This means that they potentially could be extremely profitable if they succeed.

Proponents of using market cap as the primary means of valuing companies have a well thought out argument. Stock prices tend to reflect the beliefs of investors and analysts in the anticipated earnings of a company. Higher earnings should cause traders and investors to bid up the price of the stock. Multiplying this price by the number of shares gives a comparable means of valuing one company against another.

A downside to valuing businesses this way is that it can give companies without profits high valuations. In the dot com bust at the turn of the century, technology companies that had never turned a profit were valued in the tens of billions of dollars. This in theory made them more valuable than reliable companies that had actual assets and earnings. Companies in slower growing industries are also typically valued less than they should be since their stock prices are often undervalued. Critics of this way of valuing companies suggest that more accurate measures would include the value of a company's assets, its annual revenues, or its earnings per share.

Companies whose market capitalization falls substantially below their asset value become takeover targets. This is because corporate raiders are able to buy a company for less money than they will realize by selling off its various parts, businesses, and assets separately.

Market Value

With regards to real estate, market value is the price which a real property seller can anticipate obtaining from the property purchaser in normal open and fair market negotiations. In general, appraisers value a home or other piece of real estate property utilizing a number of critical factors. When markets are volatile, such prices will vary significantly. Real estate agents may place one value on a home or other piece of real estate, yet in the end, the true property value is only what an able and willing buyer will actually pay to acquire it.

It is crucial to be aware of the market value of a piece of property individuals or businesses are selling as this ultimately sets the asking price of the real estate in question. Those sellers who are not intimately aware of this will either overprice their houses or under price them. Either of these actions will often lead to poor financial results. Not being aware of a property's true value can cause homeowners to become victims to practices of predatory lending. In this unscrupulous lending behavior, the bank or other lending financial institution will prevail upon a borrower to take out a greater amount of money than their property is really worth.

It is real estate agents or better still professional appraisers who determine most accurately the market value of a house or piece of real estate through measuring it up to other properties in the area or neighborhood which share similarities with the one in question. Real estate agents and appraisers call such recently sold area properties "comparables." They will always seek to find houses which are as alike in style, size, and location to the one they are appraising as possible.

Such properties must have sold within the prior six months to a year. According to this strategy, the professionals will similarly discern what the typical price per square foot of the houses in the area actually is. This practice by itself will not set the market price of a house, but it will give the professionals a good starting point from which to set a reasonable and viable asking price for the property.

There are also various other factors which influence a property's market value. These include the condition of the property in question as well as any improvements which the seller makes. Where a home is concerned, bathroom and kitchen renovations and updates are the main ones which will boost the selling price. Other more cosmetic appearance improvements like new carpet, fresh paint, updated light fixtures, and special window treatments will help a house to show better and perhaps sell faster, yet they will not increase the all around value of the home.

Yet it is absolutely true that the overall condition of any piece of real estate will impact its total value. Houses that boast more current and better maintained appliances and systems, roofs, windows, and even entry doors will realize a significantly better final selling price than those which offer flawed structures or outdated appliances, systems, entry doors, and mechanics.

In corporations and investments, market value is the price for which a given asset will sell in the open market. This measure of value can often be applied to the market capitalization of any company which is publically traded. Determining the market cap value is a matter of multiplying out the current price per share by the quantity of total outstanding shares.

This measure of market value is simplest to calculate for those instruments which are traded on exchanges, like futures and stocks. This is because their market prices are readily available and commonly disseminated. With over the counter securities such as fixed income securities, it can be far harder to ascertain. Yet the most difficult to determine market values are those commonly associated with less liquid assets such as businesses and real estate. This is why business valuation experts and real estate appraisers determine the market values for such assets as these.

Moody's

Moody's is a company that creates credit ratings, analysis, research, and tools which help to make markets easier to understand and more transparent for investors and clients around the world. Moody's Corporation acts as parent company to the two divisions of Moody's Investors Service and Moody's Analytics.

The Investors Service offers research and credit ratings on securities and debt instruments for a large range of companies, cities, municipalities, nations, and supra national organizations. The Analytics division provides customers with cutting edged advisory services, software, and research for economic and credit analysis and managing financial risk. In 2015 the company itself boasted a staff of nearly 11,000 individuals with offices in 36 countries that generated $3.5 billion in revenues.

The company is best known for its famous system for rating securities that they originated over 100 years ago. John Moody created this method for securities ratings back in 1909. The idea behind such ratings is to offer investors an easy to understand grading system that they can use to gauge securities' creditworthiness in the future.

Moody's Investors Services grades credit using ratings symbols. Every symbol was deigned to categorize a group where all of the elements of the credit worthiness are generally similar to one another. The company limits the system to nine different symbols. The ones with lowest credit risk start with A and gradually decrease to C to show the securities with the highest credit risk. These ratings grades are Aaa (highest possible), Aa, A, Baa, Ba, B, Caa, Ca, and C (lowest possible). Besides these the Investor's Service also adds the numbers 1, 2, or 3 to all of the classifications of ratings from Aa through Caa.

Sometimes there are no ratings given out to a company. Other times the company has ratings that have since been withdrawn. This does not mean that the issue has problems with its credit worthiness. It could be that the company placed the issue privately. There may not be enough important information available on the issuing company or their actual issue. Other times the issuing company or its particular issues are part of a group that the company simply does not rate. Finally, applications for ratings may not have been turned in to the Investor's Service or may not have been approved for one reason or another.

Ratings can also be withdrawn. It might be that the Investor's Service can no longer perform adequate analysis to update a rating. The data could be out of date so that proper judgments may not be formulated. When bonds are redeemed or called in, ratings are also withdrawn.

Moody's Investor's Service also changes the ratings it issues on securities, companies, and governments. This is because for the majority of issuers the quality of their credit improves or deteriorates naturally over time. This is why the service is interested in updating the ratings to properly reflect any changes in the strength of the issuing entities and their various obligations.

With individual issues, these ratings changes can happen at any time. When Moody's discerns that there has been a significant change in the quality of credit or that the earlier rating did not accurately reflect the actual quality of the issue, then they may intervene with a new rating. Bonds with lower ratings tend to receive more frequent changes than would bonds that possess superior ratings. Holders of any quality of bonds are encouraged to check the ratings consistently to make sure that their credit rating has not changed.

Moody's also rates sovereign countries, cities, counties, municipalities, and supranational organizations for their debt. Very few countries anymore qualify for the coveted Aaa rating since the financial crisis of 2008 and Great Recession destabilized the finances and debt positions of even some of the most dependable developed country economies in the world.

National Association of Securities Dealers (NASDAQ)

The NASDAQ is the acronym for the National Association of Securities Dealers Automated Quotation Systems, though the organization has dropped the Automated Quotation Systems part of the name as obsolete. This NASDAQ is the country's second largest stock exchange. It represents the principal rival to the NYSE, or New York Stock Exchange, which is the largest stock exchange in the country and only one larger than it.

The NASDAQ is also the largest equity securities trading market in the U.S. that is based on an electronic screen. When market capitalization, or the value of its stock per share multiplied by the number of outstanding shares, is considered, it is the fourth largest trading exchange in the world. The NASDAQ actually records a higher trading volume than does any competing electronic stock exchange on earth with its actively traded 2919 ticker symbols.

NASDAQ became established in 1971 by the NASD, or National Association of Securities Dealers. The system originally represented the successor to the OTC, or Over the Counter traded market. It later developed into an actual stock exchange of sorts. By 2000 and 2001, the NASD sold off the NASDAQ into the NASDAQ OMX Group, who presently own and operate it. Its stock is listed under the symbol of NDAQ since July 2 of 2002. The FINRA, or Financial Industry Regulatory Authority, oversees and regulates the NASDAQ stock market exchange.

The NASDAQ made major contributions to the world of electronic stock exchange trading as the first one of its kind on earth. When it began, it started out as a computer bulletin board system that did not literally put buyers and sellers in touch. Among its great achievements, the NASDAQ proved to be responsible for decreasing the spread, or the bid and the asking prices' difference for stocks. Many dealers disliked the NASDAQ in the early days, as they made enormous profits on these higher spreads.

In subsequent years, the NASDAQ evolved into a typical stock exchange through adding volume reporting and trade reporting to its new automated trading systems. This exchange became the first such stock market in America to advertise to the public. They would highlight companies that traded on the NASDAQ, many of which were technology companies. Their commercials closed out with the motto the stock exchange for the nineties and beyond, that they eventually changed to NASDAQ, the stock market for the next one hundred years.

The NASDAQ is set to become a trans Atlantic stock exchange titan with its purchase of the Norway based OMX stock exchange. This will only enhance its European holdings that presently include eight other stock exchanges throughout Europe. Besides its NASDAQ stock exchange in New York City, the group possesses a one third stake in the Dubai Stock Exchange in the United Arab Emirates. With its double listing arrangement in place with the OMX exchange, the NASDAQ OMX is set to become the major competitor for NYSE Euronext in bringing in new listings.

Net Operating Profit After Tax (NOPAT)

Net operating profit after tax is also called by its acronym of NOPAT. This refers to the potential earnings (in cash) of a corporation working under the pretense that it has no debt. This NOPAT metric is often utilized in so-called EVA economic valued added calculations. The formula for determining NOPAT is as follows: the operating income times the result of one minus the tax rate. For companies which are debt leveraged, this NOPAT proves to be a more precise and exact way of examining their operating efficiencies. As such it does not factor in the tax advantages which a number of corporations enjoy from their debt load.

Analysts and accountants consider a number of varying performance metrics when they are evaluating a corporation in which to invest. The two most frequent performance measures turn out to be sales (or revenue) and net income growth. With the revenue/sales figures, this delivers a top line performance metric. It does not say anything about the company's operating efficiency value though. Similarly the net income does include the operating expenses of a firm, yet it also factors in the net tax benefits and savings from the company's particular debt leverage.

This is where the Net operating profit after tax comes in as a useful hybrid form of alternative calculation. It permits the analysts to compare and contrast a company's performance against past metrics and other companies by removing the effects of debt leverage from the equation. This allows analysts to truly fairly measure one company against another, regardless of the two firms' net debt positions.

It always helps to consider a real world, concrete example with these complex terms. If a company's EBIT Earnings Before Interest and Taxes was $12,000 and their tax rate was 25 percent, then the calculation for NOPAT would translate to $12,000 times the result of one minus .25,(or .75). This equals $9,000 as a NOPAT. It is an after tax cash flow estimate that does not include the tax benefits of debt. For those companies without debt, Net operating profit after tax equals the same amount as does the net income after tax.

It is worth noting that analysts prefer to compare and contrast firms within the same industry when utilizing the NOPAT metric. This is because every industry has its own normal range of operating costs. Some industries' typical expenses turn out to be dramatically lower or higher than others' do.

For example, cable utilities would have extremely high operating costs associated with initially putting in, continuously upgrading, and maintaining their technology and physical hard-wired distribution networks. Soft drink businesses like Dr. Pepper/Snapple Group (DPS) have relatively low costs since they generally license out their products to other companies which produce and distribute them on their behalf.

Net operating profit after tax has other uses besides the helpful view of a company without its debt leverage being considered. Those analysts who follow and predict mergers and acquisitions utilize this NOPAT value all the time. It helps them to figure up the FCFF free cash flow to firm. This is equal to the NOPAT less any changes to working capital. It also equates to the net operating profit of the firm after taxes less the firm's capital.

These two metrics NOPAT and FCFF are commonly utilized by those types of analysts who hunt down targets for acquisition. The reason for this is that the financing of the acquiring firm will then substitute in for the present financing arrangement (their corporate debt).

Net Present Value (NPV)

Net Present Value refers to a principal profitability measure that companies utilize in their corporate budget planning process. It helps them to analyze the possible ROI return on investment for a particular proposed or working project. Thanks to the involvement of time value and its depreciating effect on dollars, the NPV is forced to consider a discount rate and its compounding effect throughout the term of the entire project.

The actual Net Present Value in an investment or business project considers the point where revenue (or cash inflow) is equal to or greater than the total investment capital that funds the project or asset in the first place. This is particularly useful for businesses when they are comparing and contrasting a number of different projects or potential projects. It allows them to draw a valuable comparison of their comparative profitability levels to make sure that they only spend their limited resources, time, and management skills on the most valuable ventures. The higher the NPV proves to be, the more profitable it is as an investment, property, or project in the end.

Another way of thinking about the Net Present Value is as a measurement of how well an investment is meeting a targeted yield considering the upfront investment that the firm made. Using this NPV, companies can also determine precisely what adjustment they need in the initial investment in order to reach the hoped for yield. This assumes that all else remains constant.

Net Present Value can also be utilized to effectively visualize and quantify investments in real estate and other asset purchases in a simple formulaic expression. This is that the NPV is equal to the Current value minus the cost. In this iteration of the NPV, the current value of all anticipated future cash flow is discounted to today utilizing the relevant discount rate minus the cost of acquiring said cash flow. This makes NPV essentially the value of the project less the cost. When analysts or corporate accountants examine the NPV in this light, it becomes easy to understand how the value explains if the item being purchased (or project being funded) is more or less valuable than the cost of it in the first place.

Only three total categories of NPV ultimate values are possible for any property purchase or project funding. NPV could be a positive Net Present Value. This means that the buyers will pay less than the true value of the asset. The NPV might also be a Zero NPV. This simply means that the buyer or project funder is paying precisely the value of the asset or project worth. With a negative NPV in the final categorization, the buyer will be paying too much for the asset technically. This will be more than the asset is actually worth. There are cases where companies or buyers might be willing to pursue a project or acquire an asset with a negative NPV when other factors come into play.

For example, they might be interested in purchasing a property for a new corporate headquarters whose NPV is negative. The reasoning behind such a decision could be the unquantifiable and intangible value of the location of the property either for visibility purposes or because it is next to the present company headquarter premises.

It is always helpful to look at a concrete example to de-mystify difficult concepts like Net Present Value. Consider a corporation that wishes to fully analyze the anticipated profits in a project. This given project might need an upfront $10,000 investment to get it off the ground. In three years time, the project is forecast to create revenues amounting to $2,000, $8,000, and $12,000. This means that the project is expected to provide $22,000 on the initial $10,000 outlay.

It would appear that the return will amount to 120 percent for a gain greater than the initial investment. There is a reason why this is not the case though. The discount rate for the time value of money has to be factored in, and this means a percentage of several points per year at least. The figure of 4.5 percent is often utilized on a three year project like this. This takes into consideration the fact that dollars earned three years from now will not be so valuable as today's earned dollars. This is why the corporate accountants will use business calculators in order to plug in the discount time value rates to figure the true NPV. Discounting by the 4.5 percent means that the project actually will return somewhere near $21,000 in terms of today's dollar value.

Net Profit

Net Profit refers to the remaining sales dollars which are left over after a firm pays for all of its operating costs, interest on debt, preferred stock dividends, and taxes. Common stock dividends are not included in the amounts deducted from the firm's aggregate sales revenue. Sometimes analysts call this type of profit the net income, the bottom line, and/or the net earnings.

A simplistic (but useful) way of thinking about this form of profit is that it is all of the money which remains after all of the expenses of the going concern are paid in full. Calculating the net income is done when aggregate expenses are subtracted from total revenue. Because these net earnings traditionally occur on the final line in an income statement, companies often refer to it as their "bottom line."

It remains true that this Net Profit is still among the most closely watched business indicators in the world of finance. Because of this, it has a substantial part in the computations of financial statement analysis and ratio analysis. Stake holders in the corporations also scrutinize this bottom line carefully since it ultimately proves to be the way they become compensated as shareholders in the firm. When corporations are unable to realize enough profits to pay their shareholders, stock prices plunge. On the other hand, when corporations are growing and in solid financial health, the more available profits become reflected in greater stock prices.

A common mistake that many individuals make is in their understanding of what net profits actually represent. Net profit is never the metric for the total cash earnings a firm realized in a certain period. The reason for this confusing fact is that income statements also showcase a range of expenses that are not cash-based. Some of these are amortization and depreciation. In order to understand the true amount of cash which corporations actually generate, investors and analysts must carefully review the cash flow statement.

In fact any changes to net profit will be constantly and thoroughly reviewed, examined, and discussed. When firms' net profits are negative or even lower than anticipated, there are a host of issues that could be causing it. It might be that the customers' experience is negative. Sales could be decreasing for one or more reasons. Expenses at the company could be out of control or simply poorly managed and monitored. New management teams may not be performing at the anticipated or promised levels.

In the end, the Net Profit will range wildly from one firm to the next and according to which industry they represent. One industry's profits will likely be substantially different from another industry's. It is not a useful comparison to make between one corporation and another since these profits are quantified in dollars (Euros, pounds, Swiss francs, or yen). It is also a fact that no two corporations will be exactly the same size by either revenues or assets.

This is why many analysts prefer to make comparisons between corporations and industries by utilizing what they call profit margin. This is the net profit of a company as a percentage amount of its total sales. Sometimes analysts and investors will also look at the P/E Price to Earnings Ratio alternatively. This widely cherished ratio reveals to considering investors what the price is (in the form of stock price) for every dollar of net profit the corporation actually generates.

Analysts still like the metric of net profit despite these limitations. A survey conducted querying around 200 marketing managers who were senior level revealed that an incredible 91 percent agreed that they believe this measurement to be very useful.

Operating Cash Flow (OCF)

Operating Cash Flow is also known by its abbreviated acronym OCF. It refers to a metric for the quantity of cash which a corporation or company's typical daily business operations produce. As such, it provides a good insight into a firm's ability to generate enough cash flow in order to either grow or at the very least maintain its existing operations. It might also prove that a going concern requires outside financing in order to fund its expansion plans.

Publically traded firms must calculate their Operating Cash Flows through employing an indirect method of calculation. This GAAP Generally Accepted Accounting Principles mandate means that they have to adjust their net income into a cash basis. They do this by making alterations to their accounts that are not cash. This includes accounts receivable, depreciation categories, and inventory changes.

In fact the Operating Cash Flow is a true representation of the cash portion of the firm's net income. This will also take into account other non-cash items thanks to the requirements which the GAAP sets out for net incomes to be done as accrual-based reporting. This means that amortization, compensation which is based upon stock shares, and incurred but as of yet not paid for expenses would be included in the calculations.

Besides this the actual net income has to be adjusted to reflect changes to working capital kinds of accounts in the balance sheet of the corporation. Especially important is the fact that any accounts receivable increases actually equate to booked revenues for which no collections have been completed. Because of this, these increases have to be taken off of the net income figure. This is partially offset at least by any reported accounts payable increases that are due but as of yet not paid, since this remains in the net income number.

Analysts have opined that such Operating Cash Flow represents the most accurate and basic form of outflows and inflows of cash as a company engages in its normal operations of the daily business. Where the health of a firm is concerned, this represents among the most crucial of metrics. Yet it most appropriately and usefully works for those corporations that are not overly complex.

The Operating Cash Flows focus on the both outflows and inflows which a corporation's principal business activities involve. This includes buying and selling inventory, paying employee salaries, and delivering services. It is important to remember that all financing and investing activities will not be included in the Operating Cash Flow. These become reportable separately. A part of these excluded activities would be purchasing equipment and factories, borrowing money, and engaging in share holder dividend payouts. Finding this cash flow number is easy by looking at the corporation's cash flows statement. This statement will break out the numbers into several categories including cash flows from operations, from financing, and from investing.

Operating Cash Flow is a very important number on a company balance sheet. Many financial analysts and investors would rather consider such cash flow measures since they reduce the impacts of confusing and opaque accounting tricks. It also delivers a better, sharper big picture for the business operations' health and reality.

Consider the following examples. When a firm concludes a big sale, this delivers a major increase to its revenues. This is irrelevant though if the firm can not collect on the money owed. It does not represent a real gain for the corporation. At the same time, firms could be producing elevated operating cash flow numbers. Despite this, they might have an abysmally low net income number if they employ an accelerated depreciation calculation or possess many fixed assets.

Permanent Financing

Permanent Financing refers to a longer term loan or debt instrument. It can also be thought of as longer term equity financing or debt. Most of the time, such long term financing becomes utilized to buy or develop the kinds of long lasting fixed assets like machinery or factories. The payoffs and contributions from such longer term assets happen over grater lengths of time. This is why long term financing makes sense in order to lessen the risks that the principle will not be paid down or off, as could be the situation with debt financing.

With longer term debt financing, money will be borrowed from a third party source so that a business can finance a particular project and the associated assets or purchases. On the other hand, longer term equity financing centers on putting up company assets in exchange for obtaining funding for particular projects and their relevant asset purchases. There are many cases where a partial ownership stake in a corporation will be offered so that the firm is able to come up with the necessary capital for the projects. Both opposing options come with their own pros and cons. This is why the owners of the company or the corporate directors will be the ones who have to decide for themselves which choice works best for their particular enterprise and scenario.

Such Permanent Financing should never be confused with shorter term financing. There are several critical characteristics that differentiate the two types. Short term financing requires that the debt be paid back in under 12 months. The opposite idea of this is the long term debt option. Such debt will offer more than 12 months and often times many years or even decades to repay it. There are many types of longer term debt. Among the most popular of these are bonds, mortgages, and loans.

Another difference between short term and long term debt lies in the repayment schedule. Short term debt is often repaid in a single lump sum repayment. With the Permanent Financing or longer term debt, these payments can be either made annually, monthly, or in a few periodic lump sum repayments.

The reasons for such debt issues is another major difference between the two types. Short term debt has a purpose of financing daily operations. An example of this might be for those firms that operate in a seasonal industry and capacity. Christmas shops are one such example. They could need short term resources in order to cover their materials, payroll, and leasing costs up to the point that their Christmas products start selling in earnest. The revenue is then utilized to pay down short term debt.

On the other hand, longer term debt is specifically utilized for buying assets that require often a few or even many years in order to pay for their cost and upkeep. A Christmas shop might want to avail itself of this type of debt facility in order to pay for constructing a bigger Christmas ornament and goods production factory. They would be able to repay the longer term loan little by little over the ensuing years. It would allow them to take advantage of the rising revenue stream and resulting profits created by the higher production output of the long term new factory facility.

It is not only businesses that can take advantage of Permanent Financing. The sovereign governments of the world similarly use longer term financing routinely to pay for their annual budget deficits. In the case of the United States, these instruments take the form of longer dated and maturing Treasuries. Good examples of these longer term debt government obligations are both 10 year and 30 year Treasury Bonds.

Prime Rate

The Prime Rate is the most typically utilized shorter term interest rate for the United State banking system. All kinds of lending institutions in the United States employ this U.S. benchmark interest rate as a basis or index rate to price their medium term to short term loans and products. This includes credit unions, thrifts, savings and loans, and commercial banks.

This makes the Prime Rate consistent around the country as banks strive to be competitive and profitable in their lending rates which they provide to both consumers and businesses. A universal rate like this simplifies the task for businesses and consumers as they shop around comparable loan products that competing banks offer. Every state in the country does not maintain its own benchmark rate. This makes a California Prime or New York Prime identical to the U.S. Prime.

Commercial and other banks charge this benchmark rate to their best customers. These are those clients who have the best credit ratings and loan history with the bank. Most of the time banks' best clients are made up of large companies.

The prime interest rate is also known as the prime lending rate. Banks typically base it on the Federal Reserve's federal funds rate. This is actually the rate that banks loan money to each other for overnight purposes. Retail customers also need to be aware of the prime lending rate. It directly impacts the lending rates that they can access for personal and small business loans as well as for home mortgages.

The federal government and Federal Reserve Bank do not set the prime lending rates. The individual banks set it. They then utilize this base rate or reference rate to set the prices for a great number of loans such as credit card loans and small business loans.

The Federal Reserve Board releases a statistics called "Selected Interest Rates." This is their survey of the prime interest rate as the majority of the twenty-five biggest banks set it. It is this publication which reveals the Prime Rate periodically. This is why the Federal Reserve does not directly set this important benchmark rate. The banks more or less base it on the target level of the federal funds rate that the Federal Open Market Committee sets and changes at their monthly meetings.

Different banks adjust their prime lending rate at the same time. The point where they change it is generally when the Federal Open Market Committee adjusts their own important Fed Funds Rate. Many publications refer to this periodically changing reference rate as the Wall Street Prime Rate.

A great number of consumer loans as well as commercial loans and credit card rates find their basis in the prime lending rate. Among these are car loans, home equity loans, personal and home lines of credit, and various kinds of personal loans.

The rates above the prime lending rate that banks charge their less then prime (or subprime) customers depend on the credit worthiness of the borrower in question. The banks attempt to correctly ascertain the risk of default for the borrower. For the best credit customers who have lower chances of defaulting, banks can afford to assess them a lower interest rate than others. Customers with higher chances of defaulting on their loans pay larger interest rates because of the risk associated with their loans not being repaid.

As of June 15, 2016, the Federal Open Market Committee voted to maintain its target fed funds rate in a range of from .25% to .5%. As a result of this, the U.S. prime lending rate stayed at 3.5%. Once per month the Federal Reserve committee meets to determine if they will change the fed funds rate.

Principal

Principal has several different meanings. It most commonly pertains to the initial amount of money that a person either invests or borrows with a loan. A secondary meaning has to do with a bond and its face value. Sometimes the word pertains to the owners of a company or the main participants in any type of transaction.

Where borrowing is concerned, this term relates to the upfront amount of any loan. It also is utilized to describe original amounts which the individuals still owe on the loan in question. Looking at a clear example always helps to clarify the concept. When people obtain a $100,000 mortgage, this Principal is the same $100,000. As the individuals pay down $60,000 of this amount, the remainder of $40,000 that is left to pay off is similarly referred to as Principal.

It is the original Principal that decides how much interest borrowers will pay. If borrowers take out a loan with an initial amount equaling $20,000 that comes with a yearly interest rate at seven percent, then they would be required to pay $1,400 in annual interest for each year that the loan remains open. As borrowers pay the monthly payments to the loan servicer, the interest charges for the month will first be paid off. What remains goes toward the initial amount which the individuals borrowed. Paying down this original amount borrowed remains the only means of lowering the interest amount that accrues on a monthly basis.

Another form of mortgage that operates differently has the name of zero principal mortgages. Bankers think of these as interest-only loans. They represent a unique form of financing where the routine monthly payments of the borrower only apply to the loan's interest. This means that the initial loan amount never gets paid down unless the borrower makes extra payments. It also translates to no equity building up in the property which backs the mortgage loan.

Because of this, financial advisors will typically not recommend these types of mortgages to home buyers as they are rarely in the true interest of the purchaser. Despite this fairly obvious assessment, there are a few unusual cases when they could work out for certain people. When a home buyer is starting out on a career path that pays very little initially but will later on earn substantially more in the not too distant future, it could be worthwhile to lock in the home price now while it is lower. Once the income increases apace, the borrowers always have the ability to refinance into a more traditional mortgage which would cover payments on the initial amounts borrowed as well.

Another scenario where these loans make sense relates to unusual and fantastic opportunities for a particular real estate investment deal. When huge returns on investment dollars can be anticipated, it is practical to go with these mortgage's far lower payments that are interest-only. Meanwhile the borrower can plow the additional monthly payment money savings into the exceptional investment opportunity.

Principal also finds use describing the first initial outlay on an investment. This does not take into consideration any interest that builds up or earnings on the investment. Savers might deposit $20,000 at a bank in a savings account with interest. After a number of years, the balance will grow to $21,500. The principal remains the original $20,000 the savers gave the bank. The additional $1,500 will be called interest or earnings on top of this initial outlay.

It is interesting to note that inflation will not change the nominal value of a loan or financial instrument's principal. Yet the effects of inflation do very much reduce the real value of the initial amount.

Private Equity Firm

A private equity firm is a company that provides capital which is not from public stock exchanges. It is instead made up of private investors and funds. They invest their money directly into private companies or public companies via buyouts. When they take over a public company in this way, the entity becomes delisted from its stock exchange.

The capital or money for a private equity firm comes from a combination of retail and institutional investors. This money can be used for a variety of purposes. Some of these include acquiring other companies, funding startups and new technologies, improving an existing company's balance sheet, or improving working capital.

Private investors who contribute money to these private equity firms must be accredited. This means they can prove by their income and assets that they can afford to tie up significant amounts of money for longer time periods. Many of these investments require substantially longer holding periods for distressed companies to be turned around. Similarly it can take years for start up ventures to reach the status of a liquidity event like an IPO initial public offering or sale to another firm.

The private equity market has grown to be powerful quite rapidly since the decade of the 1970s. Nowadays, more than one private equity firm will often work together to pool funds so that they can buy out enormous publicly traded companies. When these come together to do this it is often referred to as an LBO leveraged buyout.

An LBO provides huge amounts of funds to finance a massive purchase. Once they have completed this transaction, the private equity firms will work to improve the company's balance sheet, financial health, and profits with an eye on ultimately reselling the bought out firm to another company or spinning the company back off using an IPO.

A private equity firm commonly receives two types of income from its investors. These are performance and management fees. Many of these companies assess an annual two percent management fee for all assets they handle. On sales of bought out companies, they commonly get 20 percent of all profits made.

Investment professionals are always interested in obtaining jobs with these private equity firms. The salaries can be enormous. With only a billion in AUM assets under management, such companies will usually employee two dozen or fewer investment professionals. These companies earn millions of dollars in fees between their management and performance fees.

Medium level volumes of from $50 to $500 million in deals will earn employees salaries in excess of $100,000. Vice presidents at such companies bring in around half a million dollars' pay. Principals can easily surpass $1 million in salary. Bonuses can be on top of this when the companies realize good years.

Transparency calls began to ring out in the private equity world starting in 2015. This was because the earnings, bonuses, and incomes of practically all employees at almost all of these companies were enormous. This led a few different states in 2016 to start working on regulations and laws for a greater clarity on the inside dealings of these private equity firms. The American Congress in Washington has been resisting these efforts and trying to limit the amount of information which the SEC Securities and Exchange Commission is able to access.

Private Equity Fund

A Private Equity Fund refers to a fund that is not carried by a public stock exchange and which does not have to be regulated by the SEC Securities Exchange Commission. Private equity itself is made up of the range of investors and funds who choose to invest directly in privately held companies. They might also pursue mergers and acquisitions to cause public companies to be delisted by taking private the companies which were public.

The capital for such private equity comes from retail and institutional investors. Such funding is useful for many types of purposes. It might bolster working capital, make possible research into a new technology, provide for acquisitions of public or other privately held companies, or simply improve a given company's balance sheet.

Such private equity funds derived most of their resources from accredited investors and institutional investors. These deep pocketed entities are able to allocate enormous amounts of money into an investment (that might possibly fail) for longer term time frames. Generally these longer investment holding time frames become necessary for such private equity investments. This is because working with distressed companies or waiting on liquidity events like IPO initial public offerings or selling the private company to a public one needs time.

This private equity fund market has grown rapidly from the 1970s to date. Nowadays, funding pools can be started by private equity firms so that they can take enormous public companies private. A substantial quantity of these private equity operations engage in what analysts call LBO leveraged buyouts. With an LBO, large purchases can be affected in the markets thanks to the pooling of enormous resources. Once the transaction is completed, the private equity firms will do their very best to better the profits, prospects, and all around financial condition of the newly privatized company. Their greatest hope and plan is to resell the company back via an initial public offering or alternatively through selling the company to another larger firm.

It is worth noting that the fee arrangements of these private equity funds are different from one fund to the next. They generally start with a management fee and add a performance-based fee to the costs as well. Some firms will assess an approximately two percent management fee each year based on the value of the assets under management. They usually also get 20 percent of all profits realized when selling any companies.

When investors hand over their money to one of these private equity funds, they are throwing their lot in with an adviser that is actually a private equity firm. These funds are something like a hedge fund or mutual fund in many respects. All three of them are comprised of pooled resources that an advisor combines to utilize for investment purchases for the common good of the fund. There are differences between these types of pooled funds though.

Private equity firms will usually concentrate their efforts on longer term time framed investment possibilities. They will often look for those assets that require significant amounts of time in order to sell investments. This given investment horizon will require many times at least 10 years and sometimes significantly longer than this.

A common strategy of investing with these private equity funds proves to be engaging in minority stake investments in startups or companies which are rapidly expanding in a promising industry. Others focus solely on the previously mentioned leveraged buyouts. In either case, transparency of these funds is an issue that has been growing since 2015. The high incomes for these funds have raised questions about what they are doing with the enormous sums of money they receive.

From 2016, some states began to pursue regulations and bills that provided more clarity on what the inner workings of such private equity firms is really like. The congress has so far resisted these investigations and tried to limit the ability of the SEC Securities and Exchange Commission to access the funds' privately held proprietary information.

Prospectus

In the world of finance and investments, a prospectus proves to be a legal document. This document is utilized by businesses and institutions who must describe in great detail the type of stock or bond securities that they are issuing for potential buyers. Such a prospectus generally offers great information to investors concerning stocks, mutual funds, bonds, and even other types of investments.

The information contained in a prospectus will be reports like the financial statements of the company, a detailed description of their business, biographies of directors and other officers along with their pay packages, lists of properties and assets, and information concerning any lawsuits with which they are involved.

When stocks are first being issued as in an IPO, or initial public offering, such a prospectus is given out to the interested parties of investor prospects by brokerages and underwriters. This prospectus should always be read by an interested investing party in advance of putting capital into their security. This is especially important so that you will know the risks that are inherent in the company's business and their stock or bond issue in advance of becoming involved with their securities.

In the U.S., securities may not be offered to the public until after a prospectus has been first placed on file with the SEC, or Securities and Exchange Commission. This is a component of a registration statement. Once the SEC states that the registration is in effect, the stock or bond issuing company is then allowed to utilize the prospectus to help finalize the shares of stock or the bonds in question. The SEC examines a prospectus to ensure that is maintains the appearance of abiding by the disclosure rules.

Some corporations are allowed to work with a simplified prospectus to issue stock and bond securities. These companies must be up to date with their Form 10-K filings with the SEC for a given amount of time, keep their level of market capitalization over a minimum amount, and engage in some procedures. Some scenarios do not mandate that an offering has to be SEC registered. In these cases, a prospectus is called either an offering circular or offering memorandum.

A good example of this is the offerings of municipal securities. These turn out to be exempted from the majority of federal security laws. Such municipal types of issuers usually make up a disclosure document type that is referred to as the official statement instead. This would not offer the depth and scope of a standard prospectus, but will still contain a great deal of helpful and useful information on the particular offering.

Companies generally do not have the time to put together a prospectus entirely on their own. Since this is the case, they commonly engage the help of an issue manager who is also the underwriter of the new issue. These issue managers are also known as book running managers.

Quantitative Risk Management (QRM)

Quantitative Risk Management represents the discipline which deals with the ability of an organization to quantify and manage its risk. This scientific approach to business is becoming increasingly critical in today's world as organizations need to satisfy stakeholders who demand it.

Government regulators similarly insist on clarity within organizations now, especially regarding the amount of capital financial institutions are holding. The firm executives are hunting for the best allocation of capital. Corporations and their boards are seeking justification to control expenditures. Project managers need to be assured they will make their timelines and meet budgets. All of these individuals and entities are looking for effective QRM nowadays.

These QRM capabilities give decision makers the facilities to both analyze their applicable risk data as well as to forecast the likely positive and negative effects in the future. It provides the organization with enormous advantages. Analyses that are more dependable and finely detailed will deliver information which management requires to make superior decisions that are ultimately better informed. As the Quantitative Risk Management process yields higher quality information and becomes more easily accessible to the relevant organizational members, the decision makers are able to more effectively utilize the techniques of QRM to decrease the amount of guesswork involved in the daily decisions of their business operations.

This allows them to obtain valuable insights into possible risks, so they can estimate their overall exposure to them and discern any weaknesses in their oversight controls. It also permits them to determine how practical new services and products will be and to consider the opportunities for up selling and also cross selling of company goods, information, and services. Finally, organization leaders will be able to evaluate any degrees of variance in their company cash flow so that they can streamline and better their ultimate operations.

Quantitative Risk Management is important as every one of those activities just mentioned contains at least some degree of risk. By quantifying and considering them all using a combination of techniques such as trending, modeling, stress tests, and metric evaluations, company decision makers can create faster and more effective responses. This allows them to benefit from any uncovered opportunities and simultaneously to deal with any possible negative effects before they actually materialize and cause significant damage.

There are numerous examples of the uses of and needs for Quantitative Risk Management in business organizations. Cash flow at risk, or CFaR, represents one of the most significant drivers of business. Company leaders require effective prognoses of their future cash flow in order to firm up important decisions for the business. These include confirming or pushing off investments, reducing expenses, reinvesting capital in the business model, or choosing to reengineer their critical operations. Correctly extrapolating cash flow involves proper understanding of such underlying factors as currency changes, sales, pricing of products and services, vendor viability, and operational costs.

Value at Risk, or VaR, is another critical measurement in an organization that benefits from Quantitative Risk Management. Bigger, international, and more complicated financial institutions such as JP Morgan Chase, Citigroup, HSBC, Standard Chartered Bank, BNP Paribas, and Banco Santander have to constantly evaluate where their risk exposures are in order to appropriately allocate the correct capital amounts to be capable of absorbing losses which they do not anticipate.

Project risk management is another area where this Quantitative Risk Management can save the day. So many projects exceed their allocated budgets, deadlines, and milestone markers simply because there is not a sufficient evaluation of the variables, uncertainty, and risk involved with the project itself. This is where the process of QRM can save enormous amounts of time, frustration, and ultimately resources by delivering on deadlines and budgets.

Resource Holdings

Resource Holdings, also known as Resource Land Holdings and RLH, is a private equity firm which focuses on purchasing huge pieces of real estate which are rich in natural resources. The company's ultimate goal with these acquisitions is to sell off those parts of the properties that do not generate cash flow so that they can reduce the cost basis of the property to as nearly zero as they can. At the same time, the work to maintain and improve the cash flow of the remaining piece of property to share this out to their investors. They also enter a number of partnership arrangements with original owners so that these parties remain actively involved in the management and success of the operations. The company is headquartered in Colorado Springs, Colorado in the United States.

Resource Holdings arose in 1998 because its founders wished to provide opportunities for and to invest themselves in timber, agricultural, and mining properties and operations throughout the United States. They work with a variety of local operators, brokers, and entrepreneurs in order to invest in this range of land parcels across a wide range of asset classes which are rich in resources. As of time of publication of this article, RLH had created and managed two individually funded entities along with four different private equity funds.

The first Resource Land Fund I they capitalized with $20 million worth of committed equity. It entered its first investment back in December, 2001. Their second Resource Land Fund II they established using $51 million in equity. It purchased its initial investment in July, 2003. Their Resource Land Fund III received a larger $175 million. It obtained its first investment March of 2006. Each of these investment funds received full investment and then was closed in turn. The Resource Land Fund IV closed with $316 million in committed funds back in August of 2010.

The firm seeks out investments in land across a range of asset classes. Their primary focus has always been on regional timber, agriculture, quarry, mining, and other resource rich properties which have typically been ignored or overlooked by the massive institutional investment world. Such regional entrepreneurs that require significant capital intense investment have found that the needed funds are often not available to them as economic cycles create financial and funding challenges for these medium sized operations. In these particular scenarios, Resource Holdings appears on the scene as a life saving potential source of capital. They often invest right along with local entrepreneurs and partners.

As part of their specific portfolio of investments and property holdings, Resource Holdings owns or invests in properties across 20 different states in the U.S. spanning from Florida, to Texas, to California. At time of publication, they had 46 different properties within their various funds and portfolios. Among these were a limestone quarry in Texas, a citrus operation in Florida, timber operations in California, sand quarrying in Alabama, a large coal surface mine in the Midwest, and apple orchards in Washington state.

As an example, Resource Holdings saw that there were positively growing trends within the building stone market. They used this basis to seek out and invest with two long standing operator-owner partners of two different limestone quarries found in the center of Texas. The owners continue operating the limestone quarrying firm with RLH as the capital partner.

In another instance, the investment firm saw an opportunity to become involved in a successful Florida citrus business a few years ago. They arranged a unique sale-leaseback with the owners which guaranteed the investment company both a minimum yearly return and a profit split with the operating partner-owners. Thanks to their sympathizing and working with the various concerns of the owners, they were able to obtain a high quality property that the markets never had an opportunity to seize. The final arrangement which the company struck with the owner operators allowed both of them to sit on one side of the table to share economic objectives and interests.

Retained Earnings

Retained earnings are a component of the earnings categories of corporations. They describe the portion of a company's net earnings that they do not give out to shareholders as dividends. Instead these earnings are kept by the firm so that they can pay down debt or reinvest in their core operations and business model. Balance sheets note earnings which are retained as part of the shareholder's equity column.

There is a formula for figuring out retained earnings. It adds the initial earnings with net income or subtracts net losses from it. Dividends must then be subtracted out from these earnings as they are paid out to stockholders.

Corporations have their reasons to keep a portion of their earnings. In the majority of scenarios, they wish to invest them into segments of the market where the firm is able to build opportunities or growth. This could be by spending money for additional research and development or in purchasing new plants, equipment, or machinery. Companies can also use these earnings to purchase other firms. Such acquisitions allow them to expand their market share or product offerings in this method of non organic growth.

It is possible for such earnings to become negative. This happens when the firm's net loss is larger than the initial retained earnings. Such a case creates a deficit. The general ledger for these earnings becomes adjusted each time an entry is placed for the expense or revenue accounts.

At the conclusion of the company's accounting period, such earnings that are retained become reported. This could be in the quarterly report or the annual report. They will either continue to be accumulated and be positive, or they can shift into negative territory and be recorded as a deficit. These changes in earnings from one accounting period to the next are not directly noted. It is easy to infer them by looking at the totals of ending and beginning retained earnings for the accounting period. Increases or decreases to the accumulated totals happen because of dividend payouts and net losses or net incomes for the period.

Every period, a firm's revenues and expenses must be closed out. This is done into an income summary that shows the total net income or loss. Finally these are closed out into the retained earnings column. Net income directly boosts or decreases these earnings this way.

Dividends are the other major item that decreases the retained earnings number. Such dividends can be paid out as stock or cash. Either type reduces the earnings which are retained. This is because cash dividends come out of the net income ultimately. The greater amount of dividends that a company distributes, the lower amount of earnings it will retain. Dividend accounts are also temporary in nature and are closed out to the earnings which are retained at the end of the accounting period.

Though newly issued shares given out as dividends do not reduce the net income, they must be reconciled on the balance sheet. This is done in the accounts for additional paid in capital on the balance sheet. The earnings which are retained category decreases by the identical amount as this paid in capital column.

Return on Assets (ROA)

Return on Assets is also known by its acronym ROA. It is also sometimes called return on investment. This proves to be an indicator of a company's profitability compared to its aggregate asset base. With ROA, investors and analysts can learn about the big picture of the efficiency of an organization's management compared to the deployment of their company assets which produces earnings.

This is figured up relatively easily. To calculate the ROA, simply take the corporation's annual earnings (or income) and divide these by the firm's total assets. The final answer is the percentage amount of ROA. Other investors will do a slight variation on the formula by adding back in the corporate interest costs to the net income. This allows them to employ operating returns before the net cost of debt.

Thanks to Return on Assets, analysts and investors can learn the amount of earnings that the invested capital or assets produced. Such a figure ranges dramatically from one publically traded company to the next. Every industry's ROA varies substantially. For this reason, analysts prefer to compare and contrast the ROA primarily against the company's own prior figures or alternatively versus another company which is both similar and in the same industry.

Company assets are made up of equity and debt together. The two kinds of financing will jointly fund most corporations' various operations and projects. Because of this Return on Assets number, investors are able to discern the efficiency with which the firm converts its investable money into actual net income. Higher ROA numbers are always considered to be superior. They mean that the corporations can bring in larger revenues and earnings on a smaller amount of investment.

Consider a real world example for clarification. If Imperial Legends Strategy Games produces a net income of $2 million on aggregate underlying assets of $6 million, then it has a Return on Assets of 33.3 percent. Another company Joy Beverages may enjoy the same earnings but against a full asset base of $12 million. Joy Beverages would have an ROA of only 16.7 percent in this scenario. This means that ILSG does twice the job of converting its all around investments into profits as does Joy Beverages.

This matters because it speaks volumes of the quality of management. There are not too many managers who are able to turn over significant profits utilizing small investments.

The Return on Assets provides observers with a snapshot and analysis of a business that is distinctive from the usual return on equity formula. Consider that certain industries need to pay more careful attention to the ROA figure than other ones do. In banking, some firms managed to avoid the various banking crises of the last few decades. The ones that sidestepped the problems better than others had something in common. It was that they were more conservative based on the ROA they deployed. The more successful banks did not allow their return on assets numbers to become too unnaturally high. They did this by contemplating the underlying fine details in the loan book. Too many loans that yielded too high a return indicated that management was taking excessive risks. Yet in the business of software development firms, these enterprises are not leveraged, so this ROA comparison is less important.

An important difference separates asset turnover from Return on Assets. Asset turnover specifies that companies have sales which amount to a certain amount per asset dollar on the corporate balance sheet. Conversely, the ROA explains to investors the amount of post tax profit that a firm creates for every $1 of assets it has. This is to say that the ROA compares all of the company earnings relating to the entire resource base the company claims, including both long-term debt and the capital from shareholders. This makes the relevant ROA a strict test of shareholder returns. When companies possess no debt, then their two figures of ROA and ROE Return On Equity will be identical.

Return on Equity (ROE)

Return on equity proves to be a useful measurement for investors considering a given company. This is because it takes into account three important elements of a company's management. This includes profitability, financial leverage, and asset management. Looking at the effectiveness of the management team in handling the three factors gives you as an investor a good picture of the kind of return on equity that you can expect from an investment in such a company.

Return on equity is very easy to calculate. You can figure it up by collecting two pieces of information. You will need the company earnings for a year and the value of the average share holder equity for the same year. Getting the earnings' figure is as simple as looking up the firm's Consolidated Statement of Earnings that they filed with the Securities and Exchange Commission. Alternatively, you might look up the earnings of each of the last four quarters and add them up.

Determining share holder equity is easiest by looking at the company's balance sheet. Share holder equity, which proves to be the difference of total liabilities and total assets, will be listed for you there. Share holder equity is a useful accounting construct that reveals the business assets that they have created. This share holder equity is most commonly listed under book value, or the quantity of the share holders' equities for each share. This is also an accounting book value of a corporation that is more than simply its market value.

To come up with the return on equity, you simply divide the full year's earnings by the average equity for that year. This gives you the return on equity. Companies that produce significant amounts of share holder equity turn out to be solid investments, since initial investors are paid off using the money that the business operations generate. Companies that create substantial returns as compared to the share holder equity reward their stake holders generously by building up significant amounts of assets for each dollar that is invested into the firm. Such enterprises commonly prove to be able to fund their own operations internally, which means that they do not have to issue more diluting shares of stock or take on extra debt to continue operating.

The return on equity can also be utilized to determine if a corporation is a cash generating machine or a cash consuming entity. The return on equity will simply show you this when you compare their actual earnings to the share holder equity. You can learn at almost a glance how much money the company's present assets are producing. As an example, with a twenty percent return on equity, every original dollar put into the company is creating twenty cents of real assets. This is also useful in comparing subsequent cash investments in the company, since the return on equity percentage will demonstrate to you if these extra invested dollars match up to the earlier investments for effectiveness and efficiency.

Return on Investment (ROI)

ROI is the acronym for return on investment. This return on investment is among the most often utilized methods of determining the financial results that will arise from business decisions, investments, and actions. ROI analysis is used to compare and contrast both the timing and amount of investment gains directly with the timing and amount of investment costs. Higher returns on investment signify that the results from investments are positive when you compare them against the costs of such investments.

Over the past couple of decades, this return on investment number has evolved into one of the main measurements in the decision making process of what types of assets and equipment to buy. This includes everything from factory equipment, to service vehicles, to computers. ROI is similarly utilized to determine which budget items, programs, and projects should be both approved and allocated funds. These cover every type of activity from recruiting, to training, to marketing. Finally, return on investment is often employed in choosing which financial investments are performing up to expectations, as with venture capital investments and stock investment portfolios.

Return on investment analysis is actually used for ranking investment returns against their costs. This is done by setting up a percentage or ratio number. With the vast majority of return on investment calculation methods, ROI's that are higher than zero signify that the returns on the investment are higher than the associated expenses with it. As a greater number of investments and business decisions compete for funding anymore, hard choices are increasingly made using the comparison of higher returns on investment. Many companies believe that this yields the better business decision in the end.

There is a downside to relying too heavily on the return on investment as the only consideration for making such business and investment decisions. Return on investment does not tell you anything regarding the anticipated costs and returns and if they will actually work out as forecast. Used alone, return on investment also does not explain the potential elements of risk for a given investment. All that it does is demonstrate how the investment or project returns will compare against the costs, assuming that the investment or project delivers the results that are anticipated or expected.

This limitation is not unique to return on investment, but similarly plagues other financial measurements. Because this is the case, intelligent investment and business analysis also relies on the likely results of other return on investment eventualities. Other measurements should also be used along side the return on investment to help measure the risks that accompany the project or investment.

Wise decision makers will demand more from return on investment figures than simply a number. They will require effective suggestions from the person making the return on investment analysis. Among these inputs that they will desire are the means of increasing an ROI's gains, or alternatively the means for improving the ROI through decreasing costs.

Revenue

Revenue refers to the amount of money which firms generate in receivables within a certain time frame. It includes deductions for merchandise which is returned as well as any applicable discounts. This is also known as the gross income or sometimes the "top line" amount. Net income can be figured out by subtracting the costs from the revenue.

Analysts and accountants determine the amount of revenue simply by taking the price for which services and goods sell and multiplying this by the quantity of units or the actual amount which the firm sells. Sometimes revenue is referred to as "REVs."

There are a number of other definitions and synonyms for revenues. Some call it sales in layman's terms. Whatever name businesses and individuals refer to it by, revenue proves to be the total amount of cash which a company garners through its aggregate business activities. The price to sales ratio is one measurement in business that relies on revenues for the denominator. This contrasts with the competing measurement of price to earnings ratio, which utilizes the profits instead for its denominator.

Revenue can be figured up by several different means. It is really up to the method of accounting which companies and corporations choose to employ. With accrual accounting, sales which the firm makes using credit also count among the revenues so long as the customers have taken delivery of the services or goods. This is why investors and analysts must review the company's cash flow statement in order to evaluate how effectively a firm actually collects on the money which its customers owe it.

The other primary form of determining a company's revenues is through cash accounting. This form of accounting utilizes only sales for the revenues' quotient once the money a customer owes has been collected by the firm in question. When a customer gives the money to a corporation or company, the firm recognizes it as a receipt instead of the general category of revenues. Companies can actually have receipts that do not include revenues. This is possible if a customer were to pay for a service in advance of receiving it or for purchased goods which they have not yet received.

Revenue can also be called "top line" since income statements display them first on the report. Analysts then take revenues and deduct the expenses so that they can come up with the "bottom line," which is also called simply profit or alternatively net income.

Many times investors evaluate both a firm's net income and revenues independently of one another so that they can ascertain how strong a business' health really turns out to be. The reason for this is that net income can increase while revenues remain flat. Cost cutting can actually cause this phenomenon. This scenario is not a positive sign for the longer term growth potential for a firm.

Analysts and investors often further subdivide the revenues from a given company or corporation according to the groups which generate the money. Company accountants can also divide up the receipts of the firm into several categories of operating revenues, the core business of the firm's sales, and non-operating revenues that come from secondary sources. Such non-operating variants are typically not recurring or can not be forecast successfully. This is why these are sometimes known as one-time gains or events. Examples of this could be money gained through lawsuits, investment windfalls, or receipts from selling an asset.

Where a government is concerned, revenue refers to the receipts they obtain as a result of fees, taxation, fines, securities sales, transfers, intergovernmental grants, resource rights and mineral rights, or any sales of government assets or state-owned and -run companies which they might make.

In the world of not for profit organizations, such revenues are commonly referred to by the phrase of "gross receipts." Among the components that make up these receipts are donations from companies, foundations, and individuals; investment returns; grants out of governmental agencies and entities; membership dues and fees; and fundraising endeavors.

Sale And Leaseback

A Sale And Leaseback is also known as a simply leaseback. This arrangement involves an asset seller who first sells the asset or property in question then immediately leases it back exactly as it is from the buyer. These types of deals are fleshed out and contracted immediately following the asset in question's sale. The precise amount in payments and the specific time period to be covered are both set at this point. It amounts to the asset seller personally becoming the lessee while the buyer becomes the actual lessor under such an arrangement.

Many owners of small to medium sized enterprises (SMEs) find that they require a great deal of fresh capital in order to expand their operations. There are a number of different ways in which they can come up with such capital. Two of the more popular and better known ones are surrendering equity in order to obtain funds or taking on debt either as bonds or secured loans.

With equity, it does not have to be repaid to the provider. The cost for this is that a portion or even all of the ownership of the enterprise is surrendered. The tradeoffs for debt are that it has to be repaid one day (or in regular periodic payments). It also appears as debt on the balance sheet of the company, which may impact future opportunities for financing, debt purchases, or obtaining fresh capital via an equity offering.

Hybrid arrangements which are not either equity or debt are these Sale And Leasebacks. Instead they function more as a hybrid form of debt arrangement and product. The firm entering into the deal will not grow its debt load, yet it still manages to achieve the goal of accessing capital by selling assets. Some have referred to this as a company variation on the consumer-entered pawn shop arrangement.

Extrapolating on this example, the company in question goes down to the pawn shop and provides them with a valuable piece of property or asset. In tradeoff for this asset, the company receives an agreed upon amount of cash. The only point where this comparison breaks down concerns repurchasing the asset in question. In a sale and leaseback, no one expects that the company will attempt to repurchase the property or asset, only that they will make periodic payments in order to utilize the asset.

Consider the following example. The fictitious company Johnny Appleseed Orchards requires more funding to pay its increasing numbers of contractors and employees. It is unable to obtain funding from banks thanks to a downturn in the lending market brought on by the Great Recession and Financial Crash of 2007. The company decides it will sell half of its orchard acreage to an investment company which wishes to become involved in realizing an income stream from the sale of produce. The acreage is instantly leased back to the owner-operators of Johnny Appleseed. This benefits them if the cost to lease back the acreage is less than the interest rate and total interest payments on higher interest loans they would otherwise be forced to seek.

The most typical type of a sale and leaseback occurs with builders and those firms that have many expensive and fixed assets. This is useful when they require cash which is tied up in their costly assets to utilize for other capital needs or investments, yet they still require use of the equipment or assets so that they can continue to run their business.

Such sale and leasebacks and their arrangements also give the seller of the asset some beneficial tax deductions. The lessor gains the advantages of a stable payment and guaranteed lease arrangement which continues for a predetermined and contractually pre-set amount of time.

Such sale and leaseback deals do come with a whole different set of regulations for accounting purposes than do debt arrangements. Despite this, they are not called financing in most of the cases. This keeps them as off-balance sheet arrangements. Some analysts will therefore add on capitalized leases such as these to the category of longer term debt. They do this especially as they are attempting to gain the bigger picture view of the firm in question's aggregate debt obligations.

Securities and Exchange Commission (SEC)

The SEC is the acronym for the Securities and Exchange Commission. This Federal government agency actually governs the buying and selling of stock securities and other types of related investments. The SEC also works to safe guard investors against impropriety and fraud. They encourage the development of the market with the end goal of keeping America in the first place as the world's leading economic giant.

The Securities and Exchange Commission came into existence in 1934. The stock market crash in 1929 prompted a tremendous regulatory response where the national government observed that it had to oversee and monitor investments within the U.S. The SEC is headquartered today in Washington D.C. Its staff is comprised of five commissioners who are appointed, as well as the personnel working in eleven different regional offices throughout the country. They work together to create, amend, and enforce the laws that regulate investments in the country.

The SEC has various critical missions. Among the most significant one is their role in ensuring that the markets are transparent. To do this, they significantly regulate securities trading within the U.S. Companies are required to turn in a variety of legal financial documents during the year so that investors may obtain a true picture of the total financial health of the firm in question.

The documents are kept on file in a database that is available to the public. Anyone who is interested is allowed to inspect them by logging on to the SEC's website and working through their system of electronic documentation. The SEC has great powers that it exercises in enforcing the rules. It is able to mandate company audits if it has suspicions of illegal behavior. Those it finds in violation of its rules may be brought by the SEC to court.

In keeping with the SEC's mandate to help safe guard investors, they monitor the trading of stocks and the individuals responsible for selling them. This means that exchanges, their dealers, and all stock brokers are required to work through the Securities and Exchange Commission. They can be subjected to inspection from time to time to be certain that they are properly taking care of their customers. Consumers have the right to report practices that are unfair to the SEC directly. If you are an investor, you ought to avail yourself of the SEC's wide range of documents on the various publicly traded corporations that they keep in their database on their website.

The SEC additionally governs companies that are interested in undergoing Initial Public Offerings in order to become public companies. Such interested firms have to file a significant quantity of documents with them first. To help them accomplish this, the SEC engages a big staff. Their document database includes regulations and directions for filing such documents. Consultation help is available if companies run into difficulties.

The SEC also promotes education. If you are an investor who wants to learn more about safe investing, then simply go to their website. They have workshops and publications on the site to help all investors. This is in addition to all of the companies' documents kept on file there.

Share Consolidation

Share Consolidation refers to a reverse split. In this corporate operation, a number of shares of stock become merged together into only one single share. These share consolidations can take place either in the forms of reverse stock splits or as stock share funded buyouts.

With reverse stock splits, the corporation simply decreases the quantity of shares of its own stock available in order to increase the price per share. When a stock buyout takes place, the acquiring corporation creates more shares of its corporate stock with which to buy out the chosen target company. The target firm's shareholders then receive this newly created stock from the acquiring company in lieu of receiving cash payments for the target company shares they own.

There are a number of advantages to Share Consolidation buyouts done through stock funded purchases. The acquiring firm is able to buy the target corporation without having to deploy its own cash reserves or without getting a loan. This does not mean the transaction is free or completely without cost.

In creating the new shares, this diminishes the stock price of the buyer's shares. This can happen as investors decide that the target firm is worth less than the total number of shares which the acquirer is willing to pay. The present shareholders then own a lesser percentage of the firm and its future earnings. This is the case whether or not the value of their shares decreases or instead remains constant. It explains why many companies will instead utilize combination efforts of both cash and stock buyouts in order to successfully pay for an acquisition.

When a target firm becomes a part of the acquiring company, then its own corporate shares do not trade individually on the stock exchange any longer. One hundred percent of the target corporation's shares will be traded in exchange for the shares of the buying corporation as the transaction concludes. At this point, shares of the target firm will be delisted from all market indices they may trade in, as well as from the exchanges on which they were listed themselves. This also changes the aggregate value for the index the target company used to comprise. Managers of indices often choose to substitute in another corporation in place of the target corporation to maintain the same number of companies within the index in question.

The number of outstanding shares following the buyout will vary based on the relative values of the stock issues of both the selling and buying firms. When the shares of the seller prove to be higher priced than those of the acquirer, a greater number of shares will exist following the merger. As corporations merge their own shares in a reverse stock split, fewer remaining shares will exist following the operation or alternatively the combination.

When corporations choose to consolidate their shares utilizing reverse stock splits, this typically gives a warning that the corporation has run into trouble. The firm will quite possibly no longer be able to build up its share value via increasing its sales. This would be why they are trying to boost the share price to make it seem more valuable and expensive for the investors.

Once stock prices decline below the minimum allowed price set by the hosting stock exchange, they will be involuntarily delisted off of the exchange. This is why firms which are nearing bankruptcy may attempt to consolidate the price of their share to keep them over the threshold of this minimum price. For example, the NYSE New York Stock Exchange removes any corporation when the average price for its corporate stock drops under a dollar for any rolling 30 day long period.

Shareholders

Shareholders are companies, people, or institutions which own minimally a single share of the stock in a given company. They can also be referred to as stockholders. These stockholders are not only investors, but also the owners of the corporation. As owners, they gain the advantageous results from the firm's success. This can translate into higher stock prices, dividend payouts, or hopefully both. Should the corporation not perform well, the stock holders can similarly lose value in their investments as the stock price goes down.

There is a difference between shareholders and owners of partnerships and sole proprietorships. The stakeholders in corporations do not experience personal liability for the financial and debt obligations of the corporation. Should the company in question fail, creditors can not attempt to secure payments or assets from the stockholders as they might be able to do from owners of entities which are privately held.

Corporations with shareholders have another important difference from other structures of businesses. They depend on their executive management and board of directors to handle the day to day operations. This means that the stock holders do not have much control over the daily operations of the company.

Shareholders may not have much involvement in the company's decisions, but they still have important rights. These are specified by the corporation's bylaws and charter. One of these is the right to go through the company records and financial books. Another is to sue the company for officer and director committed mistakes. Even common stock holders have the right to vote on important corporate decisions like whether to agree to a potential merger or on the makeup of the board of directors.

Shareholders have what may be their most important right when a company goes into liquidation through dissolution or bankruptcy. They have the rights to regain a representative amount of the recovered proceeds. They are in line after the secured debt holders including bondholders, preferred stock holders, and creditors, all of whom have precedence over the common stockholders.

Stock holders have several other rights which they enjoy. They receive a part of dividends which their company announces. They also gain the privilege to attend in person the annual meeting of the corporation. Here they are able to learn more regarding the performance of the firm. They can also choose to sit in on the meeting using a conference call. If these common stock holders are not able to or interested in going to the annual meeting, they can instead choose to vote through the mail or online using a vote by proxy. All of these rights which belong to preferred and common shareholders are detailed in the corporate governance policy.

A great number of corporations elect to create two classes of stock. These are common and preferred shares. The majority of stock holders purchase and hold common stocks since they are more of them and they are less expensive than preferred shares. Unlike preferred stock holders who are due to receive dividends every quarter, common shareholders must wait on the board of directors to decide if and when they will be paid a dividend in a given quarter. The directors must decide if this is an appropriate way to utilize the corporation's funds.

Preferred stockholders lack the voting rights of common shareholders. They do receive higher dividends on a more frequent basis. Their payments have to be paid at least yearly and their dividends are also guaranteed. For investors more interested in creating a reliable annual income from investments, preferred shares can be a very helpful tool.

Standard and Poor's (S&P)

Standard and Poor's is a global ratings agency that is also responsible for the S&P and Dow Jones indices in the stock market. Besides providing ratings on companies and products, they also rate governments' sovereign credit ratings. This company is based in the United States but has 26 offices throughout the globe. The corporation has shortened its name from Standard and Poor's Ratings Services to S&P Global Rating as of April 28, 2016.

The history of Standard and Poor's goes back over 150 years. Today they provide market intelligence that is high quality and well respected. They offer this in the form of their well known credit ratings, global research, and thought leadership. The company operates primarily as S&P Global Market Intelligence and S&P Dow Jones Indices.

Their division S&P Global Market Intelligence proves to be among the world leaders in delivering research and information on a variety of asset classes. They provide this with thought provoking analysis via a number of advanced platforms. Every year the company gathers more than 135 billions individual points of data in the pursuit of this goal. They cover 99% of all the market capitalization in the world. Standard and Poor's wants to be more than just the provider of financial data and intelligence. They are looking to be a creative force for transparency, growth, and the provision of value in the world's capital markets.

Each day this division of the company gathers, scrubs, analyzes, and interprets enormous amounts of data and content. They take this raw information and transform it to intelligence investors can act on covering industries and companies in the worldwide financial markets. Standard and Poor's Global Market Intelligence offers not only data but also valuable insight that helps readers to make more educated and intelligent investment and business decisions that impact the future.

This division boasts several core beliefs. These are relevance, accuracy, timeliness, and completeness. The group proves to be a foremost purveyor of analytics, news, research, and information to a variety of groups around the globe. Beneficiaries of this information include corporations, government agencies, universities, and professionals.

The solutions and data which lead the industry come from their subsidiaries SNL Financial and S&P Capital IQ. These combine to put together data from individual sectors and the comprehensive market with news and analytics. The tools that result allow the group's clients to perform a wide variety of functions. They can track their performance, identify ideas for investments, generate alpha, grasp dynamics of the competition in an industry, determine credit risks, and produce valuations.

This division boasts over 10,000 employees operating in 20 countries around the globe.

The other principal division of Standard and Poor's is the S&P Dow Jones Indices. This group turns out to be the biggest international source for concepts, research, and data on indices. It counts among its legendary financial indicators the Dow Jones Industrial Average and the S&P 500 indices. It has been working with these indicators for more than 120 years to create forward thinking market solutions which help to meet needs of both retail and institutional investors.

They began with launching the Dow Jones Industrial Average in 1896 and later produced the S&P 500 in 1957. This has made them an engine in many of the most critical financial creations of the 20th century. They now offer in excess of 1 million different indices that run the spectrum of many different asset classes throughout the world. The company claims that more assets have been invested in different products that are based on their indices than with any other company on earth.

Stocks

Stocks are financial instruments that are issued by publicly traded corporations. These shares of stocks prove to be the tiniest portion of ownership that you can acquire in a company. Even by owning a single share of a company's stock you are a small part owner of the firm.

Owning shares of stock gives you the privilege of voting for the underlying company's board of directors, along with other critical issues that the company is considering. Should a company decide to distribute earnings to share holders as dividends, then you will get a portion of them.

With the ownership of stock, your liability in the company is only limited to the value of your shares. This means that should a company lose a lawsuit and be forced to pay an enormous fine or judgment, then you can not be made to contribute to it. The company's creditors also can not pursue you if the company runs into financial trouble and goes bankrupt.

Two different types of stock shares exist. These are common shares and preferred shares. The vast majority of shares that are issued are common stock shares. These are the shares that members of the public hold most of the time. They come with full voting rights and also the possibility of receiving dividends that the company pays out.

Preferred stocks come with fewer voting rights but give preferential treatment for dividend payment. Preferred stock issues are paid out before common share dividends. Companies that offer preferred stock typically pay dividends on both classes of shares anyway. Preferred stocks also have a higher claim on the assets of a company if it fails.

Liquidity is a feature of stocks that should always be considered. Common stock shares are almost always more liquid than are preferred shares. Large companies offer the greatest amount of liquidity in the trading of their stocks. Because of the depth of the stock markets, you are able to purchase and sell the shares of practically all companies that are publicly traded at any time that the exchanges are working.

When you purchase a stock, you are looking for two different kinds of gains. Cash flow or passive income with stocks comes from the dividends that they declare and pay out. Capital gains appreciation is realized when you buy a stock at a lower price than the price that you get when you later sell it. While cash flow dividends are smaller payments that are realized on a generally quarterly basis, capital gains turn out to be larger one time returns made when you sell the underlying stock shares investment. At this point, you would no longer own the stock and you would have to purchase another stock in order to work towards cash flow gains from dividends, as well as other possible capital gains.

Strategy

Where businesses are concerned, strategy proves to be both the scope and direction that a business pursues over a longer term time frame. Strategy gains a business or other organization advantages through optimally deploying and utilizing all types of resources in competitive environments. Strategy is utilized to fulfill the needs that markets experience and to live up to the expectations and anticipation of the share holders in the firm or stake holders in the organization.

Strategy covers many components of a company. It pertains to the direction, or place that a firm is trying to arrive at over a longer time frame. Strategy explores the markets that are most effective for businesses to become involved with, as well as the types of activities that they should pursue in these markets, known as the scope of a business. Strategy seeks to determine what advantage a business can acquire, or how it might operate more efficiently and effectively than the various competitors in the markets.

Businesses are also interested in a number of other elements with strategy. They are concerned with the resources that they will need to compete in these markets. Resources for a business can include facilities, technical abilities, contacts, finance, specific skills, and particular assets. Companies also look into strategy as it pertains to the external environment of the business and its abilities to compete effectively. Finally, a firm must consider the wishes and expectations of the share holders in the business with their strategy.

Strategy can be found on three main levels of a business or organization. These run from the entity at the highest level on down to the individual employees who work within the company or group. Corporate strategy is the macro level. It deals with the entire scope and purpose of a business in achieving the expectations of share holders. Investors are commonly involved and consulted with in the development of corporate strategy. Corporate strategy is typically outlined specifically within the corporate mission statement.

The different business units also have strategy, referred to as Business Unit Strategy. This level of strategy worries about the ways that the company is competitive in specific markets. Strategic decisions at this view involve choices and ranges of products, the ways of gaining an advantage over the competition, satisfying the business' customers, and creating and discovering different opportunities on which the business or organization may capitalize.

Finally, operational strategy works with the ways that all parts of the company in question are arranged to work together in order to provide both business units and corporate strategy direction. With operational strategy, processes, resources, and people are concentrated on in particular.

Strategy of a business or organization is handled and created in the processes of strategic management. Strategic management simply goes through the thought process to make strategic decisions. There are three core parts of strategic management. These are strategic analysis, strategic choice, and strategy implementation.

Structured Finance

Structured Finance refers to the possibility of and procedures for issuing loans because of a reliable history of strong corporate cash flow. Instead of using assets for a loan's collateral, the funds are given out based upon the past history that shows a consistent cash flow in the business of the borrower. This cash flow will provide for the orderly and on- time pay back of the loan principle and interest. This type of financing is usually opted for when the more traditional methods either fail or are simply not practically available to a business.

It is also fair to say that structured finance proves to be an intricately involved and even complex financial instrument. This vehicle permits big companies and financial institutions such as banks to access complicated means for financing their needs. Such needs often will not be good matches for traditional financial products.

This structured finance has grown dramatically from the middle of the 1980s decade. It has evolved and expanded since then to be a significant player in the financial universe. Classic examples of such finance are CDOs collateralized debt obligations, CBOs collateralized bond obligations, synthetic financial instruments, and syndicated loans. Alongside CBOs and CDOs, there are also fairly new instruments like CMOs collateralized mortgage obligations, CDSs credit default swaps, and even hybrid forms of securities which may involve elements of both equity and debt instruments.

In fact it is most often corporations which find themselves in need of this structured finance funding. Many times they discover that a typical loan or even conventional instrument of finance (like corporate bonds) simply will not adequately meet their needs. Sometimes this is because the transaction needs to be discretionary and discreet. In order to accomplish this, creative solutions utilizing riskier instruments are employed.

The reality is that traditional types of lenders do not commonly offer such structured finance solutions and products. It is often up to investors to come up with the major cash infusions for organizations or businesses when such financing is required. Another interesting feature of these products is that they usually can not be transferred. This simply means that they can not be altered from one form of debt to another as with a standard loan.

On an increasing basis and frequency, governments, corporations, and financial intermediary organizations utilize such structured finance securitization programs. They are often deploying these to help manage risk, expand their reach of the business, develop one or more financial markets, or create new means of funding projects. In such scenarios, employing structured finance turns cash flows into lump sum payments. It also has the side effect and consequence of changing the liquidity of financial books and portfolios.

It is the process of securitization that actually creates these complex financial instruments. The magic of this process is that it creatively combines various financial instruments and assets into a single package. These repackaged instruments are rated according to a few tiers. The tiers then get sold on to investors. The advantage to this is that it encourages and fosters liquidity in markets and for businesses.

A typical example of the process of securitization is the MBS Mortgage backed security. When individual mortgages are grouped into a single pool, the issuer gains the ability to break up the large pool into various component pieces. They do this according to their risk of default. Smaller pieces can be sold off to investors, often for a better and more advantageous price by parts than the whole pool would fetch alone.

Utilizing structured finance is often appealing to a company that may lack significant physical assets which they can pledge as collateral. Yet they may possess a substantial base of clients as well as a documented, consistent history of both billing to and payments from their customers. Many times investors will loan money to these kinds of corporations. This is often true even if the companies are small. Investors will generally loan the company money on this basis for a better interest rate than a traditional bank loan would cost the firm to obtain. It also is a faster process with less administrative paper work than a typical business loan from a bank.

Subordinate Financing

Subordinate financing refers to that type of debt finance which ranks behind the primary finance. It is second in importance and position to debt that senior or secured lenders hold. This is important when a default occurs, as it determines who gets repaid first from any bankruptcy proceedings or foreclosure. The term signifies that senior lenders who are secured will be repaid before the debt holders that are subordinate.

Lenders who participate in this subordinate financing take on greater risk than the lenders considered to be senior. This is because they have a lower claim on the business or property assets. Sometimes this type of corporate finance is comprised of both equity and debt financing. A lender would be interested in this because it would offer them potential stock options or warrants that would reward them with extra yield as a means of compensating for the greater risk they take.

Where consumer borrowers and loans are concerned, subordinate financing would be a second mortgage. It takes second priority below the original first mortgage. First mortgages have the property to secure their loan and the debt. While nearly every mortgage is backed by the underlying property, first mortgages receive special seniority ahead of subordinated mortgages. This means the senior mortgage lender is repaid first in a foreclosure. With mortgages, subordinate financing could be a mortgage that is 80/20. In this case, the first mortgage would be 80 percent while the second mortgage that was subordinated represents 20 percent.

This means that only the lenders which are first mortgage holders are likely to get at least a portion of their money back if a borrower defaults in general. Should a borrower only default on the subordinate mortgage, this lender is able to foreclose on the property to regain its principal. Subordinated lenders could work to make their mortgage the senior one and then foreclose. They could do this by buying out their borrower's first mortgage. Afterwards, they could choose to subordinate the original first mortgage so that their once second mortgage became senior in the foreclosure.

Consumers should think carefully before participating in subordinate financing to obtain their houses. There are several disadvantages involved.

Home owners will usually have to write two different mortgage payments each month if they do. They will also typically pay a higher interest rate on the second mortgage since these rates are usually greater than the first mortgage rates. There are also often two different loan fees, costs, and even discount points when first and second mortgages are used. Finally, this type of finance will often lead to a greater monthly payment when the two are combined than only one mortgage payment would.

The main reason that a home buyer would be interested in employing subordinated financing to purchase a home is because an 80/20 mortgage would not require them to come up with any down payment. It might also eliminate the need to pay for PMI private mortgage insurance which can be a substantial component of the monthly mortgage payment. This would depend on how the mortgage financing was originally structured.

Consumers will generally require a high credit score of minimally 700 in order to qualify for this subordinated financing. When borrowers have two mortgages, it will likely be impossible to obtain a home equity loan or line of credit at a later time.

Takeover

A takeover is a corporate event where a company chooses to acquire another firm in an effort to gain full control over the target firm in question. They often do this by buying a majority percentage of the firm's outstanding shares.

If such a move is successful, the company which is acquiring the target obtains control over and responsibility for its target firm's holdings, operations, and debts. If the target firm proves to be a publically traded stock company, then the company which is acquiring must place an offer to buy all of the outstanding shares of the target company.

There are several different types of takeovers in the world of business. Welcome takeovers are those like mergers and acquisitions. They typically proceed calmly as the two companies involved in the situation consider it to be a positive end scenario for all. The opposite type of takeover is known as hostile or unwelcome takeover. These often turn out to be aggressive since the receiving party does not willingly or voluntarily participate or even give its consent.

Hostile takeovers are exactly like they sound. The firm which is doing the acquiring may resort to underhanded tactics. Some of thee include a dawn raid. In this clever maneuver, a predatory firm purchases a large portion of the company's stock at the immediate opening of the market. This leads to a target firm losing control over its company before it even is aware of what is occurring. The target company's management and board of directors could choose to staunchly resist these unsolicited efforts via such defenses as taking a poison pill. Poison pills are where the shareholders of the target firm buy additional shares at a discounted price in order to dilute the holdings of the acquirer, causing the takeover to become potentially prohibitively expensive.

There are various reasons that a company would pursue a takeover. This is practically the same end result as an acquisition. Companies can perform like a bidder by attempting to build up their market share or create larger economies of scale which will aid the company in lowering its overhead so that it can boost its profits.

Firms which are the most attractive types of takeover targets are those which possess a unique advantage with a specific service or unique product. This includes smaller firms with profitable services or products but inadequate financing. Another similar company that is geographically near might decide that by combining their forces they could boost efficiency. Other examples are companies which are viable but that have to pay too high an interest on their debt which might be effectively refinanced for a better rate if a bigger and more powerful firm with superior credit ratings acquired it.

A few years ago, ConAgra tried to engage in a friendly takeover to acquire competitor Ralcorp. As the first advances were spurned, ConAgra demonstrated it would instead go the route of a hostile takeover. Ralcorp retaliated by instituting a form of poison pill strategy. ConAgra was not to be so easily outmaneuvered. They upped the ante by proffering $94 a share. This amounted to significantly more than the going rate of $65 per share for Ralcorp at the time the initial acquisition talks began.

Ralcorp declined and beat back the hostile attempts; though in the end the two companies came back to the negotiating table the next year. Eventually the deal succeeded via a friendly strategy as ConAgra paid $90 per share. At this point and time, Ralcorp had finished spinning off its division Post Cereal. This meant that the final price per share offering from ConAgra amounted to substantially more than the prior year's original offer.

Tax Accountant

Tax accountants are professionals who help clients with finances. One of their main tasks is to prepare tax returns for individuals and businesses. They complete taxes for local, state, and federal levels. These agents can do this because they have great knowledge of governmental regulations and business rules. The Internal Revenue Service established tax accounting with the section Title 26 of its Internal Revenue Code.

Tax accountants also perform a variety of other functions. They help their customers minimize the amount of taxes owed. They assist them in meeting tax filings and requirements. Accountants also update their clients on any changes to the tax code that will impact their business. When there are government audits or disputes over taxes, companies turn to their tax accountants for representation to help resolve them.

Tax accountants' work schedules are different than those of many professionals. This is because much of their business is seasonal. From mid April thru end of December, they keep busy with typical work weeks. Starting in January through mid April, these professionals see their work hours go up dramatically. The first four months of the year they are doing individual and business tax returns for clients.

Becoming a tax accountant requires significant amounts of education and licensing. These professionals generally need bachelor's degrees either in accounting or a related field. Business administration is another major that individuals can take to become an accountant. It makes a good base for a master's degree in accounting. Other master's programs that help with this line of work involve taxation, auditing, business statistics and calculus, or financial planning.

The professional qualification that sets accountants above many of their peers is the CPA. To obtain the official Certified Public Accountant status they must put in another 30 educational hours and obtain experience in accounting. Finally, accountants take an exam to gain this designation. Having a CPA credential with their state board allows them to file financial reports with the Securities and Exchange Commission.

Each state has its own requirements for the CPA license. One hundred and fifty semester hours of college or university credit is usually necessary. Most states also require a candidate to demonstrate minimally two years work experience in the field.

The American Institute of Certified Public Accounts is the governing body that administers the CPA exam. After candidates have met the other educational and experience criteria they may take this. Gaining the certification is not the end of the process. CPAs are usually required to stay caught up with various continuing education courses. Otherwise they will not be allowed to keep their designation.

There are several questions that business owners should ask before hiring a tax accountant for their enterprise. It is good to know the types of clients these professionals count. Finding one that understands their business is important. Companies also need to make sure a potential accountant is available all year round.

Finally, companies should determine that their potential financial planning company has real experience dealing with the IRS. Sometimes CPAs are a more impressive designation. This does not give them the experience that an Enrolled Agent has with the IRS. The Federal Government actually certifies EAs precisely to handle taxes. Another advantage that EAs have is that many of them have been IRS agents. As such they possess real and valuable experience in performing and handling business and personal tax audits.

Term Loans

Term loans refer to those loans a bank makes to a business or corporation for a set amount of time. These loans come with either a floating or a fixed interest rate and a pre-arranged schedule for repayment. There are numerous banks that offer such term loan programs to businesses so that they can access the funds they need for monthly operating expenses. Many times such a small business will utilize the cash they receive from this kind of a loan in order to buy equipment or other forms of fixed assets that they need for their production or manufacturing process.

Term loans are utilized for either working capital, purchases of real estate, or equipment purchases. These must be paid back in a time frame ranging from a single year on up to 25 years from issue. Payment schedules will either be quarterly or monthly. The maturity date will also be fixed on the loan. Actual interest rates could be pre-set or could vary with the floating interest rate benchmarks. Obtaining this kind of a loan will need appropriate collateral to be posted.

The approval process is exacting and extensive in order to lower the chances of default on such a loan. Small businesses which are established and that possess solid financial statements will find such loans to be appropriate for their situation. Banks will be more likely to approve them if the business is able to make a good faith down payment on the loan. This helps to lower the aggregate loan cost by reducing interest amounts and to decrease the minimum quarterly or monthly payment dollar amounts.

Funding amounts for these common commercial loans can range from $25,000 and higher. Bank loan officers usually subdivide such term loans according to one of two different categories. These are intermediate and long term loans. With intermediate loans, the loan maturity date is typically under three years. Such loans will commonly be paid back in monthly time-frame installments. There can be balloon payments due as well. Businesses expect to pay them out of their cash flow. The American Bankers Association states that repayment will typically be tied to the asset which is being financed and its useful life.

Conversely, longer term loans will last for more than three years and extend on up to ten or even 25 years long. The assets of a business will often serve as collateral for these bigger commitment loans. Usually either quarterly or monthly payments will come due. Businesses repay these installments utilizing either their cash flow or company profits.

Such longer-term commitment loans will generally come with clauses that restrict the number of other financial commitments the firm may assume in the form of debts, officers' salaries, and dividend payouts. Sometimes they will mandate that a given percentage of company profits must be put off to the side in order to pay back the loan.

While there are countless ways a business could deploy the resources from a term loan, some are more appropriate. The smartest ways to use them are through important capital improvements to the business, construction projects, large investment in capital, or buying other businesses. Working capital is another sensible use for such a loan.

The rates for these types of loans are typically competitive and not expensive relative to other forms of borrowing. They commonly cost approximately 2.5 percentage points over the prime lending rate for those loans which will be shorter than seven years. For the ones that are longer-term than this, around 3 percentage points greater than prime rates is normal. There will also be fees for such loans that usually amount to around one percent. Construction loan fees are often higher.

Too Big To Fail

Too Big To Fail refers to the disturbing but proven concept that some businesses have become so enormous and systemically important that the jurisdictional government has no choice but to save them from failing with whatever means necessary. The governments feel they must deliver material assistance to the firms in order to prevent a catastrophic rogue wave effect from reverberating across the entire economy.

The simple explanation for how a company can be so important to an entire economy is this. When such an enormous firm fails, all of the companies that count on it for parts of their revenue can also be compromised and fail, as well as its debt holders and ancillary services providing companies that work with the failing massive firm. Jobs then become eliminated en masse. For this reason, the expenses involved with a simple bailout or government backed guarantees of the mega corporation are significantly less than the cost of overall widespread economic failures. It explains why governments will often opt for the bailout as the less expensive answer to the moral problem.

Too Big To Fail especially pertains to commercial banks and financial services firms. These financial companies are so critical for the United States' and other Western economies that it would create havoc and spread financial ruin if they declared bankruptcy. Because of this, the American and British governments especially opted in the Global Financial Crisis of 2008-2009 to spare the banks and other financial service firms.

They saved the bank creditors and holders of counter party risk. As an unwished for side effect, they allowed the managers and company board members to keep their enormous salaries and incredible bonuses. Throughout the last years of the 2000's, the United States' Federal Government doled out approximately $700 billion in order to shore up such critical failing corporations as Bear Stearns, AIG, and the major banks which stood on the edge of financial ruin.

It was investors' total evaporation in confidence of the major financial institutions that led to their near-downfall back in the years 2008 and 2009. Especially the investment banks ran into trouble as they had become unbelievably leveraged (to the tune of from forty to one and eighty to one) when suddenly their mortgage loan-based assets and derivatives plunged in value as the subprime mortgage crisis spiraled out of control. Both stake holders and creditors quickly began to have doubts in their financial solvency as their balance sheets crumbled.

The defining moment in the Too Big To Fail crisis erupted when the government did not step in to prevent Lehman Brothers investment bank from failing. This has become widely known as the "Lehman moment." As widespread chaos erupted in the financial markets, regulators suddenly became painfully aware that these largest companies were so intricately connected that it would take enormous financial bailouts in order to stop literally half of the U.S. financial sector from collapsing.

Once the bailouts had intervened to save the major Too Big To Fail investment banks, only two remained standing. Even the survivors Morgan Stanley and Goldman Sachs were both forced to convert to traditional commercial banks so that they could be backstopped by the FDIC. Bear Stearns was effectively wound down, Lehman's skeleton was bought out by Barclays of Great Britain, and once-mighty Merrill Lynch became a subsidiary of Bank of America. The shadow banking industry had all but disappeared overnight.

The government then attempted to address the issues of Too Big To Fail financial firms. The U.S. Congress passed the Dodd-Frank Wall Street Reform and Consumer Protection Act of 2010. The idea was to create restrictions which would make it far more difficult for such conditions to flourish again. They hoped to sidestep having to extend other bailouts in the future.

The Act made the financial institutions create forms of "living wills" so that their plans are in place in order to rapidly liquidate assets if they have to file for bankruptcy. An internationally based consortium of financial regulators came up with a new set of rules in November of 2015 to force the major global banks to raise their capital by $1.2 trillion more in additional debt funding which they are able to convert into equity or write off if they suffer catastrophic losses again.

Trade Credit

Trade credit refers to special financing terms which are many times given to a business by a supplier. This situation arises when a business buys supplies or goods and the financial officer or owner of the vendor agrees to provide either all or half of the purchased order on credit. In the case of half on credit, the balance half would become payable on delivery of the merchandise to the business.

When businesses receive a half order trade credit, they have several possibilities for paying for the balance on delivery. If they have ample resources, they can simply pay with cash. Otherwise, they can borrow the money to pay for the other balance on the inventory. This is why such credit remains among the most critical means of lowering the amount of working capital smaller businesses especially require. It is even more common and necessary with retail operations.

Suppliers normally extend such trade credit to a purchasing business once they have been a regular client for anywhere from 30 days, to 60 days, to 90 days. This trade credit has the advantage of being interest free. An example of this concept helps to make it clearer. Perhaps a supplier ships the Great Sweater Company knitted hats. The bill might normally be due within thirty days. Since Great Sweater Company enjoys these special credit terms, they would have an additional 30 days to cover the cost of the knitted hats which the vendor supplied.

When companies first start a new business, it is difficult to obtain such credit from the suppliers and vendors. In fact they will initially require each order to be paid by either check or cash on delivery. This will be the case until the new business demonstrates that it can successfully pay its bill in a timely fashion. It is a common practice in the business world. For those startups that need to raise money to make the operations work in the early days, it is important for them to be able to negotiate some form of this credit with their suppliers. It becomes easier earlier if the business owner can provide a well-developed financial plan.

It is important for businesses to properly utilize this trade terms credit. When they become trapped in the mentality of it being a necessary means of permanently financing the operations, then the business is in trouble.

Instead it should be viewed as a useful source of funding for covering shorter term and smaller needs. This credit is not really a longer term solution to the funding problem.

For businesses who do not avoid this trap, they often times become heavily committed to working with the supplier who generously extends such trade credit terms. The end result of this is that the business is not able to choose a more aggressively competitive supplier that provides better prices, more timely deliveries, and/or a higher quality product because they do not offer such generous credit terms for their buyers. There is a trade off for everything in business.

It is important to realize that trade credit is rarely free. Every supplier may have its own terms. Yet most of them will provide a significant cash discount for those businesses that pay their invoices in 10 days or less. The same as cash price may be for 30 days. By waiting for the 30 days to pay the invoice, it is costing the business the two percent discount. If a business chose to do this for 12 months a year, it would mean the merchandise was costing an additional 24 percent versus the price of paying the 10 days same as cash terms.

When a business pays after the 30 days credit expires, most vendors charge from one to two percent interest in penalties. By being late for a year, this could cost an additional from 12 to 24 percent. This is why effectively utilizing trade credit means that a business will need to plan intelligently ahead so it does not lose cash discounts consistently or pay late fee penalties needlessly. Little details like this separate successful businesses from ones which fail.

Troubled Asset Relief Program (TARP)

The Troubled Asset Relief Program is also known by its clever acronym the TARP. This represented a series of national relief programs which the United States Treasury Department developed and administered. They did this to attempt to restore stability to the American financial system, to rebuild economic stability and growth, and to forestall housing foreclosures after the 2008 Global Financial Crisis and Great Recession wrecked the national and Western portion of the global economy. The idea was to buy up threatened firms' equity and toxic assets so that they could continue to operate and make loans.

In the first round, the Troubled Asset Relief Program provided Treasury with an mind boggling $700 billion of purchasing ability with which to purchase the dubious and at that point entirely illiquid MBS mortgage-backed securities as well as additional assets. They were to buy these from systemically important banks and financial institutions with an eye on rebuilding the shattered liquidity of the stricken money markets. It was the congressionally approved Emergency Economic Stabilization Act they passed on October 3rd in 2008 which allowed them to develop the program. With the Dodd-Frank Act for banking reforms, the Congress reduced their $700 billion amount of authorization down to a still-impressive $475 billion.

The series of events that led to this de facto bank bailout originated from the freeze up of the worldwide credit markets that ground to a screeching halt in September of 2008. This became worse as a few of the systemically important financial institutions like American International Group, and the GSE government sponsored enterprises Freddie Mac and Fannie Mae became victims of intense financial trouble. Lehman Brothers' went bankrupt which nearly overthrew the global financial system. At the same time Goldman Sachs and Morgan Stanley altered their charters to evolve into commercial banks which provided them with the backing of the FDIC Federal Deposit Insurance Corporation. This did stabilize the attacks on their two market capitalizations and shore up their capital positions, though it required some time to have effect.

It was with the Troubled Asset Relief Program that the government through the U.S. Treasury was finally able to buy up the root of the crisis, the

Mortgage-backed securities. In decreasing the possible unknown toxic asset losses from the financial institutions which held them, they saved the banking system in not only the United States but likely the entire Western world.

Critics of the Troubled Asset Relief Program called it the largest bank bailout scheme in the history of the world. Without these cash infusions into the important national banks throughout the U.S. though, they would have been unable to continue operating at all. When the program had successfully stabilized the banking system and the too big too fail, systemically all-important banks, and the market had sufficiently calmed down, TARP was allowed to expire on October 3rd of 2010.

Treasury utilized the TARP funds wisely and well. They deployed some of them to make loans, others to invest in companies in need of cash infusions, and still more to guarantee toxic assets like the MBS. They received bonds or shares off of the collapsing financial companies and banks in consideration for this accommodation. The first program was known as the Capital Repurchase Program. In this initiative, Treasury purchased preferred shares of stock in eight major banks. These included Citigroup, Bank of America/Merrill Lynch, Goldman Sachs, Morgan Stanley, Bank of New York Mellon, Wells Fargo, J.P. Morgan Chase, and State Street Bank.

The banks had to provide the government with a full five percent dividend return which had to increase to nine percent in 2013. This gave the banks huge incentive to purchase back their own stock from Treasury before the conclusion of the five year windows. Then-Treasury Secretary Hank Paulson understood the government would make money off of the program in the end as he believed the stock prices of the banks would rebound at least somewhat by or before 2013.

Four other groups and entities would have collapsed without additional help from the Troubled Asset Relief Program and Treasury. Each of these received either direct cash infusions via preferred stock purchases or loans. AIG (the largest insurance company in the world) received $40 billion. Various community banks obtained a collective $92 billion. A number of these did fail in spite of this help. The American Big Three car makers got $80.7 billion collectively. Bank of America and Citigroup also received an additional $45 billion between them. TARP also loaned out $20 billion to the sister TALF program which the Federal Reserve managed.

Though critics heavily maligned the government for saving the banking system and national banks, the bailout did not cost the government anything by the time it had been concluded. In fact, by May of 2016, the banks had paid the government back all of their principal (collectively, despite some failing anyway) plus $25 billion in profits for a total repayment of $275.04 billion.

UniCredit Bulbank

UniCredit Bulbank proves to be the biggest bank in the Republic of Bulgaria. Until 1994, this state-controlled and -operated bank bore the name of the Bulgarian Foreign Trade Bank or BFTB. It was in 2007 that the UniCredit Bulbank became formed when Bulbank, Hebros Bank, and Biochim merged together as individual subsidiaries of UniCredit Group from Italy.

Bulgarian Foreign Trade Bank first arose in 1964 in its headquarters of Sofia, Bulgaria. The at the time completely state-owned and -founded bank held an initial paid in capital of 40 million Bulgarian leva when it opened. This proved to be a large sum of capital in this day and age. At the time under the heyday of the communists in Bulgaria it specialized in foreign finance and foreign trade payments.

The bank realized that to effectively pursue foreign trade and finance, it needed several well placed good international branches. The bank then began to open important representative offices in London, Vienna, and Frankfurt throughout the subsequent decades. In 2015, the operation boasted substantially greater assets amounting to nearly 9 billion Euros and 2015 era equity of nearly 13 billion Euros.

Once Communism collapsed in Bulgaria during the successful national coup in 1989, the country established the Bank Consolidation Company in 1991 to operate the state- controlled banking sector and to help with the eventual privatizing of the various national Bulgarian banks. BCC owned 98 percent of the share capital of Bulbank at the time. It became the first Bulgarian bank operation to change over to international SWIFT codes. This helped it to massively improve its transaction reliability and operational performance as a direct result.

The bank's eventual privatization from 1998 to 2000 saw UniCredito Italiano gain control of 93 percent of the capital shares while German based re-insurance giant Allianz obtained another five percent of the remaining shares. Bulbank then sold its majority stakes in Corporate Commercial Bank and minor stakes in United Bulgarian Bank and HypoVereinsbank Bulgaria.

Bulbank has continuously worked on the merger of operations and branches between the old Bulbank offices and Hebros Bank and HVB Bank Biochim since UniCredit made the decision to merge the HVB Group back in 2005. The group was renamed UniCredit Bulbank officially at this point.

The same Chief Executive Officer has overseen the company's massive successes since the year 2001. This towering figure in Bulgarian banking and finance is Mr. Levon Hampartzoumian. He heads UniCredit Bulbank still as of end of 2016 in its second decade of existence in the present foreign owned-form of the financial institution.

Part of the leading in Bulgaria success that UniCredit Bulbank has consistently enjoyed in recent decades stems from the wide range of clientele they effectively serve. They offer bank checking, current, and savings accounts, insurance and investment products, land and home mortgages, and financing and credit for individual clients, private banking customers, small businesses, large corporate clients, other financial institutions, and even Bulgarian government and other public institutions as well.

UniCredit Bulbank is not only by far and away the largest bank in Bulgaria by branches, deposits, and assets; it is also a heavily award-winning financial institution. In 2016, it received the honors of "Bank of the Year" from the Association Bank of the Year and "Best Bank for 2016" from Global Finance Magazine. It is known as the "Best Digital Bank in Bulgaria for 2016" per Global Finance Magazine. Focus Economics ranks it as the "Most Precise Overall Economic Forecast for Bulgaria." Forbes Magazine labeled it the "Most Innovative Bank in Bulgaria". It received the "Best Bank in Bulgaria" designations from EMEA Finance Magazine and K10's Kapital Newspaper annual ranking. Global Finance Magazine called UniCredit Bulbank the "Best Trade Finance Bank in Bulgaria" in 2016, as did Euromoney Magazine as well.

Unsecured Debt

Unsecured debt refers to a kind of loan that does not have any underlying asset which is backing it. This means that if the borrower defaults, the lender has no valuable property to seize against the loan's repayment. Such debt has a wide range of examples. These include credit card bills, utility bills, medical bills, and other forms of credit or loans which a financial institution offered without requiring any backing collateral.

These debts are extremely risky for lending institutions. The creditors will be forced to sue in an effort to collect their principal should the borrowers choose to not pay back the full amount of their obligations. It is not only personal bills which can be unsecured. Unsecured debt also includes business debts. Because the risk of default is considerable for the lenders, they usually charge higher rates of interest. This is a proverbial double edged sword. Since the higher rates make the financial burden heavier for the borrower, it can literally push them into default in an ironic self-fulfilling prophecy.

Borrowers have the ability to eliminate their unsecured debt. They can do this in the bankruptcy courts of the United States. The results will be that their debts are either discharged or restructured (in the case of businesses especially). Such an action will have consequences for the borrowers. They will find it harder to get unsecured loans in the future.

There are some important differences between unsecured debt and secured debt. Debt which is secured is backed up using a valuable asset. This could include the vehicle for which the loan is made, or the real estate for which it is provided. The official name for this is collateral. The legal terms in secured loans permit the lender to simply seize its underlying collateral which guarantees the loan if and when the borrower defaults on the payments. Secured debts cover a range of loans. These include title loans that vehicles secure and real estate or home loans that the property secures.

Naturally borrowers have far more to lose personally when they default on such secured loans than on any unsecured debts. This is because the loss of the borrower proves to be the gain of the lender in the respect of the collateral. Since this kind of debt turns out to be significantly less risky on the part of these lenders, they are happy to provide a more competitive interest rate, especially as measured against the rates on unsecured debt.

When a person does not make good on their pledge to repay on an unsecured debt, creditors will go through a number of steps. They first contact the borrower in an effort to recover payment. In the event that the creditor and borrower are unable to come to agreement on a revised repayment schedule, then the creditor moves on to the next steps in the process.

They will do one of several things. They might report the delinquent borrower to one of the big three credit reporting bureaus. They could also sell the delinquent debt on to a debt collection agency which will aggressively pursue debt collection. Finally, depending on the state in which the borrower resides, the creditor could choose to file a lawsuit in an effort to force repayment of the debt.

There are states such as Florida which do not allow legally forced collections of debt. These places protect the consumers from aggressive debt collection methods such as court ordered debt restitution. In other states, when creditors file debt collection law suits in the federal or state courts, the courts can decide to force the borrowers to pay back their unsecured debts utilizing certain available resources or assets.

Corporations also receive loans which are unsecured debt. When such debt issues are being rated by the bond ratings agencies, they will typically provide that issue with a lower rating. One example surrounds the Meta Financial Group which issued unsecured debt in 2016. The KBRA Kroll Bond Rating Agency determined that this senior unsecured debt deserved an only BBB+ bond rating because it was unsecured. This is relatively low, since junk bond ratings are BB. Highest ratings from this company were AAA ratings.

Meta Financial was fortunate to receive the BBB rating though there was no underlying asset backing the debt. This was due to the company's strong quality of assets, healthy liquidity profile, and positive capital ratios on a risk-weighted basis. Had the issue been instead secured debt, then the bond rating agency likely would have delivered an A or better rating.

US Trust

U.S. Trust today is the Bank of America Private Wealth Management division. It existed as an independent U.S. Trust Corporation from 1853 through 2000. At this time Charles Schwab and Co. acquired the bank and trust. They later sold it to Bank of America back in 2007. U.S. Trust today provides (as it has for two centuries) its clients with wealth structuring, investment management, and lending and credit facilities.

U.S. Trust has its headquarters in New York City on 114 West 47th Street in the United States. The firm counts more than 100 branch offices throughout the country across 31 different states plus Washington, D.C. They work to provide their ultra high net worth clients with specially tailored solutions and resources that help meet their needs for credit and banking, investment management, and wealth structuring. Teams of advisors serve the clientele through a wide variety of financial services. Chief among these offerings are financial and succession planning, investment management, specialty asset management, philanthropic asset management, customized credit products, family office services, family trust stewardship, and financial administration.

U.S. Trust arose in 1853 as a State of New York chartered bank. This makes it the original and also oldest such trust company within the United States. The new venture had the backing of a combination of wealthy investors who poured a million dollars into the firm which was called United States Trust Company of New York at that point.

Among the first board of trustees were thirty different influential and important New Yorkers. This included founding investor New York City Mayor Joseph Lawrence from the Bank of the State of New York who became bank trust president. Secretary of the trust went to United States Life Insurance Company of New York's John Aikman. Among the other important founders were industrialist, inventor, and philanthropist Peter Cooper; Marshall Field the department store founder; President Shepherd Knapp of Mechanics National Bank of the City of New York; and steel and iron manufacturer and railroad developer Erastus Coming.

The company became founded to serve clients of individuals and institutions as a trustee and executor of their money. This proved to be an innovative concept as trusts had not been fully conceived of at this point. It only took till 1886 for the firm to be well-established as a stable and highly regarded financial institution.

Thanks to this growing reputation, by the middle of the 1800's, the company had acquired a roster of super rich clients. It served a significant role in a number of nationally and internationally important construction projects like the Panama Canal and national American railroads. A great number of the firm's corporate clients floated securities to help finance such building project initiatives. The trust got to play the part of corporate trustee in the projects. Such a boom in enterprising and industrial projects aided the business in expanding into the management of personal trusts for the super rich as well. By the 1880's and 1890's, the firm counted such prestigious and ultra high net worth individual as William Waldorf Astor, Oliver Harriman, and Jay Gould.

The company successfully managed to survive and thrive despite a range of damaging financial crises in the last half of the 1800s and the early 1900s. In 1928, it counted over a billion dollars in trust assets. It stood well above its vastly smaller rivals. Thanks to the company's emphasis on stability, it managed to ride out the 1929 stock market crash and resulting decade long depression.

The company thrived by introducing additional specially tailored personal services in the next few decades. Among these were advising its ultra wealthy clients and families on careers, private schools, and universities for their kids. By 1958, U.S. Trust had begun its earliest ads in the newspaper society pages of The New Yorker. It was also advertising in the Metropolitan Opera and New York Philharmonic Society programs at this time.

Despite restructuring in the 1970s, 1980s, and 1990s, the company still became a takeover target by Charles Schwab and Co. in the year 2000. It ceased to be an independent prestigious outfit of nearly 150 years long at this point.

Valuation

Valuation refers to the method for ascertaining the present worth of any companies or assets. A range of techniques exist to decide this value. When analysts assign values to a firm, they consider the corporation's capital structure, the firm's management, and the potential of future earnings as well as the various assets' market values.

Securities' market values will ultimately be decided by the amount that buyers will voluntarily pay to sellers. This assumes that the two sides willingly choose to engage in the transaction. As securities become traded on exchanges, the sellers and buyers together set the true market value for the bonds or stocks in question. There is also the idea of intrinsic value. It means that the believed value for securities centers on either future earnings or another characteristic of the company that is not dependent on the going market price of the relevant security.

It is critical to understand the value of an asset in order to begin to make smart decisions for the organizations or the investors. They can not determine how much to pay or accept in takeover bids or investments, decide on which investments to include in a portfolio, determine how much and how to finance operations, or decide on dividends as part of running their operations without this foreknowledge.

The central concept behind valuation proves to be that investors, accountants, and analysts are able to engage in reasonable and realistic estimates in value on the majority of assets. This allows them to place values on financial and physical assets. It will always be the case that some kinds of assets are simpler to value than are other ones. Valuation details are not the same with every asset either. Uncertainties concerning the estimates of value will also be different with various assets. Yet in the end, what remains constant are the central principles for valuing assets.

There are basically three separate approaches for valuing any asset. The first method is using discounted cash flow valuation. Following this method of assigning value means that the asset's value must be correlated to the current value of the anticipated future cash flow for the asset in question.

The second means is relative valuation. In this method of determining asset value, The given asset value may be estimated by considering the relative pricing of like assets which have characteristics in common. Important characteristics in this consideration are cash flows, earnings, sales, and book values.

The third method analysts call claim valuation. This method works with pricing models of options in order to determine a value for the assets which have characteristics in common with such options. Each of these three attempts to provide values will often provide varying value estimates on the assets. This is why valuing models always provide their explanation for why they valued an asset in a given way at a different value from the rival other two models for valuing. It makes it easier for economists, investors, accountants, and analysts to choose the best model for valuing a particular asset.

Discounted cash flows prove to be a very popular method for assigning value to many financial or company held assets. Analysts and investors will work primarily with the outflows and inflows which the asset in question generates with this method. They must discount the cash flows with an appropriate discount rate to effectively value the assets based on future anticipated cash flows.

This discount rate adjusts for the future interest rates, inflation time value on money, and investor-required returns. When a corporation purchases a new machine, they will first contemplate the purchase price cash outflow and measure the anticipated cash inflows of the new asset. Whether they are inflows or outflows, they must all be discounted down to a current value so that the firm can come up with an NPV Net Present Value. When the NPV turns out to be positive, it makes sense for the corporation to go ahead with the investment into buying the given asset.

Venture Capital

Venture capital refers to the process of investors purchasing a portion of a start up company. Firms or individuals that engage in this are called venture capitalists. They pour money into a firm that offers a high rate of growth but that also contains high risk. The typical venture capital investment time frame generally proves to be from five years up to seven years. Such investors anticipate getting a profit back on their investment through one of two ways. Either they hope to sell their stake in an Initial Public Offering to the public, or they hope to sell the company outright.

Investors who involve themselves in venture capital investments often wish to obtain a certain percentage of the company's ownership. They might also request being given one of the director's seats. This makes it easier for the investors to ask to be given their funds back either through insisting that the company be sold or reworking the deal that they made in the first place.

Venture capitalist investments are comprised of three different kinds. One of them is early stage financing that might be broken down into seed financing, first stage financing, or start up financing. Seed financing means that a tiny dollar amount of venture capital is paid to an inventor or other entrepreneur who wants to open a business. This might be employed to come up with a business plan, do market research, or bring on a good management team.

First stage financing is the type needed as companies look to boost their capital so that they can begin full scale operations. Start up financing instead is venture capital distributed to a business that exists for under a year. In this stage, a product will not be on the market already, or will only just have been put on the market for sale.

A second type of venture capital investments is known as expansion financing. Expansion financing is comprised of both bridge financing as well as second and third stage financing. Bridge financing refers to investments that only receive interest and are short term. They are mostly employed for company restructurings. They might also be utilized to cash out early investors.

Second stage financing proves to be investment money for the purpose of growing a company already up and running. While such a company may not yet demonstrate actual profits, it is producing and selling merchandise. It also possesses inventories and accounts that are expanding.

Third stage financing is investments that venture capitalists make in companies that have at least broken even on costs or are even starting to demonstrate profits. In this case, venture capital is employed to grow the business further. For example, third stage financing could be utilized to develop more or better products, or to purchase needed real estate.

Still a different popular version of venture capital investing is known as acquisition financing. In this type of venture capital, the investment goes into gaining a stake in or the entire ownership of a different company. Management could also choose to use this venture capital to buy out yet another business or product line, whatever its development stage proves to be. They might acquire either a public or a private company in this way.

Visa

Visa Inc. proves to be an enormous American-based multinational financial services operation which is headquartered in Foster City, California. The corporation is a successor company to a pioneer organization in the world of all-acceptance credit cards. Its electronic fund processing and transference occurs all over the inhabited world, typically through the unmatched Visa-branded debit cards and credit cards.

Interestingly enough, unlike many of its smaller competitors, Visa does not issue any of its own cards, establish fees or interest rates for consumers or businesses, or even offer credit to anyone. Instead they simply deliver payment products which are Visa branded to financial institutions that then brand their own credit cards. This allows the third party financial institutions and banks to provide debit cards, credit cards, pre-paid credit cards, and cash accessing programs to their own various clients.

Nielson Report issued a 2015 report that followed the credit card industry. They determined that Visa Inc.'s worldwide network, called Visa Net, handled an incredible 100 billion transactions that year. These had a volume for the year of $6.8 trillion.

Visa maintains operations on every inhabited continent. It is accepted on all 6 continents and most inhabited islands of the world. Their impressive volumes of transactions process through Visa Net. They have two separate fortress-like secure facilities that process these global operations and transactions. These are the Operations Center East, found near Ashburn, Virginia; and the Operations Center Central, found in the area of Highlands Ranch, Colorado. Each of these two key data centers for world finance is massively fortified to protect against any combination of terrorism, crime, cyber-crime, and natural disasters. They are able to function independently of one another. The Visa Inc. company is even able to run them from externally placed utilities in an emergency.

Both of the centers are capable of running as many as 30,000 different transactions at the same time. They can process a staggering 100 billion computations per second. Naturally cyber-security and fraud are major issues to these two financial data center of the world. To this effect, each processed transaction is run against 500 independent variables. Among these are 100 different fraud-detection protocols. Examples of these are the individual spending patterns of the customer involved, the location of the merchant running the transaction, and the geographical location of the customer in question. Only after the 500 variables and 100 fraud protocols pass muster will any single transaction be accepted. This is an unparalleled level of financial security in the realm of credit and debit cards.

The name Visa came from the mind of corporate founder Dee Hock. Hock felt that the word Visa could be recognized around the globe instantly in a number of different languages throughout numerous countries. He believed it gave a connotation of universal acceptance as well.

Back on October 11th of 2006, the company Visa declared that it would merge businesses and transform into a publically held company via an initial public offering. For the restructuring to work as an IPO, Visa decided to merge several of its sister outfits Visa USA, Visa International, and Visa Canada into a single company. Meanwhile, they spun off Visa of Western Europe into an individual standalone company. Its member banks own this European operation and also gained a minority stake in the newly-issued shares of Visa Inc.

The IPO deal was so massive that over 35 different investment banks worked on the offering, many of them as underwriters of this huge Initial Public Offering. This IPO became the single biggest Initial Public Offering in the history of the United States when it initially raised $17.9 billion at once. When the underwriters of the IPO decided to exercise overallotment options, they bought another 40.6 million shares in total. This increased the aggregate number of IPO shares to an astonishing 447 million. The final proceeds amount from the IPO then amounted to $19.1 billion. Today Visa trades on the prestigious New York Stock Exchange NYSE with the stock symbol of V.

Voodoo Economics (Reaganomics)

Voodoo Economics is also known as Reaganomics. The term was originally used by President George H.W. Bush (Bush the Elder) to refer disparagingly to the economic policies of his predecessor President Ronald Regan. Ironically President Bush served for eight years as the vice president under Ronald Regan after he made those remarks.

Before eventual President George H.W. Bush served as the VP of President Reagan, he considered his one-day running mate's economic policies the Voodoo Economics as unorthodox and ineffectual. This was because Ronald Reagan loved supply-side economics, wanted to cut back taxes on corporate and personal income, and planned to restrict taxes on capital gains.

The more popular term for the so-called Voodoo Economics changed into Reaganomics over time as these economic policies became wildly successful. The policies of the United States' fortieth president who served from 1981 to 1989 were considered experimental at the time. President Reagan suggested that the economy (which was under a terrible recession since the time of President Jimmy Carter) could be massively stimulated by unconventional methods. These would eventually include massive and across the board tax cuts, significantly lowered social spending, greatly increased spending on the military, and the financial deregulation of American markets. President Reagan introduced these measures to combat the lengthy era of economic and financial stagflation which had started back under President Gerald Ford in the year 1976.

While pre-Vice President George Bush the Elder intended for the term Voodoo Economics to be negative and harmful, the later adopted phrase Reaganomics served both critics and proponents of the policies of President Reagan. This set of policies came from the ideas of trickle down economics theory. Such an idea believed that by decreasing taxes, particularly those on companies, the government could stimulate the economy and increase economic growth. The concept held that as corporations found their expenses were reduced by federal policies, these savings would eventually find their way on down into the remainder of the national economy. This would then cause a boost in the growth rate.

As part of his plan, President Reagan unleashed a four part strategy to lower inflation and to increase the job and economic growth. He started by cutting back the federal government's spending on programs which were domestically based. Next he cut taxes for especially businesses, but also on individual investments and personal tax rates. Third, he decreased the burdensome regulations that handcuffed corporations and companies. Finally, he fostered a lower growth rate of money within the U.S. economy.

While President Reagan did manage to lower the domestic program spending, he over compensated for it with his boost to military spending. This caused a financial net deficit and grew the U.S. debt burden during both of his four year terms. He did effectively slash the highest individual income tax rate down from an eye watering 70 percent to 28 percent. Corporate tax top rates declined from 48 percent down to 34 percent.

Reagan moved on by cutting through all of the restrictive economic regulations which President Jimmy Carter had enacted. He also finally put an end to the dreaded and stifling price controls which still remained on natural gas and oil, cable television, and long distance phone service. During his second term, President Reagan encouraged a Federal monetary policy which helped to finally stabilize the American dollar versus major foreign currencies.

Towards the close of the second term of President Reagan, he had increased the Federal government's tax revenue base from $517 billion of his incoming year 1980 to $909 billion by his final year of 1988, effectively almost doubling it. He had cut inflation back to four percent, and he had pushed down the unemployment rate to under six percent. Economists and politicians may continue to spar regarding the ultimate impacts of the Reaganomics/ Voodoo Economics, yet no one argues that it did bring on what has become among the strongest and longest lasting eras of continuous prosperity in the history of the United States. From the years 1982 to 2000, the DJIA Down Jones Industrial Average increased in level by almost 14 times. The economy increased the job base by 40 million new ones during those heady years.

Wall Street

Wall Street is a physical street that is seven blocks long and runs from Broadway to the New York East River. It lies to the south of the Manhattan borough of New York City. The street is incredibly significant because it has played host to a number of the most important financial entities in the United States.

The city originally got its name because of an earthen built wall that Dutch Settlers of the city erected in 1653 to ward off an anticipated invasion of the English. The street's importance grew so rapidly that before the Civil War in America this was already known as the nation's sole financial capital. In the district of Wall Street there are many important buildings and headquarters.

The street contains the Federal Reserve Bank, the New York Stock Exchange, the International Commodity, Cocoa, Sugar, Coffee, and Cotton Exchanges, and the NYSE Amex Equities. There are also numerous municipal and government bond dealers, investment banks, trust companies, and insurance and utilities' headquarters located here. A great number of the major American brokerage firms have their headquarters in this financial district.

Because of Wall Street, New York City is sometimes called the most important financial center in the world as well as the greatest and most powerful city economically. Investors find the two biggest stock exchanges in the world as measured by market capitalization here in the NASDAQ and the New York Stock Exchange. A few other significant exchanges also make or made their headquarters here. These are the New York Board of Trade, The New York Mercantile Exchange, and the one time American Stock Exchange.

In the 2000's there were seven major Wall Street firms here. These included Lehman Brothers, Merrill Lunch, Morgan Stanley, Goldman Sachs, Citigroup Inc, JP Morgan Chase, and Bear Stearns. Several of these companies failed outright or had to be sold at urgently distressed prices to rival financial companies in the Great Recession that ran from 2008-2010. Lehman Brothers had to file for bankruptcy in 2008. The U.S. government made JP Morgan Chase buy Bear Stearns. The Treasury and the Federal

Reserve then forced Bank of America to purchase Merrill Lynch.

The catastrophic collapse of this many major financial firms dramatically downsized Wall Street with massive re-structuring. It proved to be especially severe for the economies of New York City and the surrounding states. This was because the financial industry in New York produced nearly a quarter of all income in the city. It also amounted to about 10% of all tax revenue for the city and 20% of taxes for the state of New York. City and state government revenues and budgets suffered dramatically from this loss of revenue for years. The Boston Consulting Group estimated in 2009 that as many as 65,000 jobs were permanently gone as a result of the financial crisis.

This city and financial center has grown to become a global symbol for investment and high finance. Movies have been made about it including two with the same title Wall Street and its sequel Wall Street: Money Never Sleeps. The financial district has become a part of modern mythology in many ways starting back in the 1800s.

The street emerged as a hated symbol of the greedy robber barons who took advantage of workers and farmers to the populists of the 19th century. When times were good it represented the way to get rich quick. Following such terrible stock market crashes as 1929 and 2008 the street looked like the home of financial manipulators who could crush major international companies and even derail the economies of entire nations.

Weighted Average Cost of Capital (WACC)

Weighted average cost of capital (WACC) refers to a calculation of the cost of a capital for a company. It involves every category of the company's capital being weighed proportionately. Each source of capital for the relevant corporation will be considered by this designation. This means that preferred and common stock, bonds and all types of longer-term debt will all be included in the WACC calculation. It will go up with the rate of return on equity and beta increases. When the WACC increases, this means that the risk has increased while the valuation for a firm has decreased.

Calculating weighted average cost of capital requires taking each part of the capital components and multiplying them by their appropriate proportional weight. These individual calculations are then added together to come up with the WACC.

Companies can finance their needs through one of two main types of funding. This is either via equity issuing in the form of primarily stock shares or through debt issuance as with bonds. This measurement actually weights appropriately the two main forms of corporate financing, with each weighted according to its relevant utilization in a particular situation. It allows companies and analysts to decide how much every dollar they are financing will cost them in interest, making it imminently practical.

The reasons this is important are evident. The holders of equity and lenders of a corporation will demand specific minimal returns on their capital or lent money they have delivered. This is why WACC proves to be so useful. It shows the cost of capital for both the stake holders (as equity owners) and the lenders (as the debt holders). This means that both groups will be able to understand the levels and amounts in returns they can anticipate receiving. Another way of looking at the weighted average cost of capital is that this is the opportunity cost of any investor for assuming the risk which investing in the corporation entails.

A firm's WACC represents the all around return on capital for the company. This means that the directors of the corporation will commonly utilize the numbers internally to make appropriate decisions for the organization. Such decisions might include evaluating opportunities for expanding the business or the financial practicality of engaging in an acquisition or a merger.

It is helpful to consider examples to best understand this complex concept of weighted average cost of capital. Assume that a corporation is a money pond. Money comes into this pond out of two separate streams which are the sources. These streams represent the equity and the debt of the company. Money which the daily business operations bring in does not count as another source. The reason for this logic is that once a firm pays down its debt, any remaining money that they do not pay out as dividends or for share buybacks becomes what analysts call retained earnings held in trust for the shareholders.

Consider lenders that want eight percent return for their funds they loaned to a given company. At the same time, the stakeholders possessing the stock share may want a minimum 16 percent return on their investments or they will not hold onto the shares of the company. This means that the projects which the corporation funds using its money pond will need to provide an annual recurring return of 12 percent so that both their lenders and equity holders will remain happy. This 12 percent represents the weighted average cost of capital.

Going back to our original example of the money pond, if it contained $100 in debt holder money and $100 in investments from shareholders, the company might invest $200 in one of its projects. They would then require an annual return of 12 percent total, or $24 from the project funded by the pond. This would mean that $16 of this return was for the share holders while $8 of the total return was for the debt holders.

Western Union

Western Union proves to be a world-leading provider of global payment options and services. They help customers who range from individuals and families, to small businesses and not for profit NGOs, to international corporations. The company does more than simply help businesses and individuals to move money; they help national and international economies to expand and communities to experience a more prosperous and better life.

For the full reporting year 2015, Western Union transferred more than $150 billion dollars between customers and businesses around the globe. The firm boasts an impressive 500,000 different agents' locations, with more than 100,000 of their own ATM's and kiosks found around over 200 different countries and territories of the globe. They are constantly seeking to find smarter and better, more innovative and cutting edged means of sending money utilizing mobile, digital, and retail channels by providing a vast range of options for convenient pickup or payout to help their consumers and businesses with their cash needs.

Western Union is a major player in the world of currency translation as well. Their transactions happen throughout over 130 different currencies between more than a billion individual bank accounts around the world. They average an impressive 31 different transactions for every second (per the year 2015).

By simply going down to a retail outlet or utilizing the Western Union website or mobile app, customers are able to move money from almost any location to almost any other domestic or international location, from one currency to almost any other, and all in a matter of minutes. This helps their customers to be able to send money out to their family members or friends in almost every corner of the globe. They can offer financial support and encouragement, empower an education or entrepreneurial opportunity, or simply honor someone for a special accomplishment or occasion.

Their flagship service for individuals who wish to send money across the globe is called WU Connect. This international cross border system allows for peer to peer sending of funds to over 200 different nations and territories around the world. Pickup can be arranged via a wide variety of approved bank accounts, Western Union physical agent locations, and select mobile wallets.

Business customers also have access to a toolbox full of helpful services. The main category for this is the Western Union Business Solutions platform. This enables businesses to navigate their way through the challenging global economy. They can avail themselves of risk management, international payments, and cash management tools. More than 100,000 medium to smaller business clients, financial institutions, NGOs, and educational institutions are able to effectively transact in and make payment across national borders and through widespread geographical time zones.

Larger businesses and multinational corporations which require help in hedging international currency movements for the future are able to take advantage of their Leverage Forward Contracts. These help them to lock in an attractive current day exchange rate for specific time frames that extend up to 12 months out from the present date. This assists multinational corporations and big businesses in safeguarding their profit margins against currency movements over the short to medium term time frames. The WU system allows clients to place market orders in any time of the day or night. They can even set up a monitoring order to wait for a targeted advantageous exchange rate, whether or not they are sitting at their desk in the physical office or not.

The businesses can also avail themselves to the services Western Union offers to manage a company's exposure to foreign currency. Risk can be first identified and then addressed using a four step risk management protocol. The company maintains a staff of well-trained and knowledgeable specialists who are able to help set goals and develop a simple yet effective currency hedging plan to reduce and control currency exposures while protecting the important margins of profit.

Wholesale Banking

The concept of wholesale banking pertains to those banking services which are done between merchant banks or commercial banks and various other financial institutions. This form of banking services has to do with bigger bank clients like enormous corporations or other financial institutions. In contrast, retail banking concentrates on individual clients and small businesses. Such particular banking services cover financing of working capital needs, currency conversions, large trade transactions, and a range of alternative and specialized banking services.

There are so many different avenues which wholesale banking covers. This specialized department within the mega banks handles capital markets products, integrated credit, and a range of different advice and guiding for risk management, funding needs, and investment products and services for international and domestic major corporate clients. Such products and services run the gamut of structured transactions, specialized finance, credit structuring, loan syndications, project finance and securitization, merchant banking, wholesale equities, and public sector financing of infrastructure projects.

Among the many different types of wholesale banking clients are corporations which are medium sized to large, institutional investors and clients, pension funds, governmental departments and agencies, and other global banks and financial institutions both domestic and abroad. The services which they often need in day to day operations include equipment financing, cash flow management, large loans, trust services, and international merchant banking.

The concept also relates to lending and borrowing between larger institutional banks and other financial organizations. Such lending mostly goes on in the interbank market and revolves around huge sums of money in practice.

The majority of commercial banks function as such merchant bank operations, providing wholesale banking services besides the more usual retail customer banking services. It makes it more convenient for those customers who require wholesale banking services, as they will not be required to track down and go visit a specialized financial institution. Rather they are able to deal with the same bank which handles the customer's individual retail banking needs.

The most understandable means of comprehending this wholesale banking phenomenon is to draw parallels with a discount superstore chain such as Sam's Club or Costco. These outfits trade in such enormous quantities that they are able to feature special deals and lower fees per dollar of sales. For bigger institutions or organizations, this makes it advantageous for them who possess high dollars of assets and business banking transactions to participate in this banking wholesale instead of going the more traditional retail banking customer services route.

As an example, many businesses possess numerous locations throughout the country. They often times require a solution for their cash management, which wholesale banking can easily provide. Technology companies are an especially relevant business line for this type of banking. Perhaps an SaaS firm owns 10 sales offices throughout the U.S. It might be that every one of its 50 sales department members needs their own access to the company's corporate credit card. The company owners also insist on every one of the regional sales operations maintaining at least $1 million in cash reserves on hand. This amounts to $10 million worth throughout the various offices combined. Companies with these type of needs will be too big for the traditional format of ordinary retail banking.

The owners of this company might instead contact a significant sized bank and ask for a corporate account which will handle each of the company's financial accounts. These services function as a facility which will provide discounts to the company in exchange for meeting a minimum dollar level cash reserve requirements as well as a minimum level of monthly bank transaction requirements. It is in fact easy for the SaaS company to hit such targets each and every month. This is why the company will seek out such a corporate facility in order to properly consolidate together each of its financial bank accounts so that it may effectively reduce its total fees. This makes so much more sense for a larger company than instead having 10 different regional bank checking account and 50 separate retail bank corporate credit card accounts.

Yield

In business and finance, yield is the word that states the quantity of cash that comes back to a security's owners. It is measured independently of variations in price. It proves to be a percentage of total return. It is used for measuring the return rates of fixed income investments, such as bonds, bills, strips, notes, and zero coupons; stocks, including common, convertible, and preferred; and various other insurance and investment hybrid products like annuities.

Yield can mean different things in varying situations. It is sometimes figured up as an IRR, or Internal Rate of Return, or alternatively as a ratio. Yield describes an investment owner's entire return or a part of the income.

The end result of the many differences in yield is that they can not be compared one against the other. This is because they are not all the same from one branch of finance and investments to another. You could see numerous different formulas for figuring up yield used by different investments and groups.

Bonds are a classic example of this. Nominal yield is also known as coupon yield. This proves to be the face value of a bond divided into the annual interest total. Current yield instead is those interest payments over the bond's price on the spot market.

A yield to maturity is the internal rate of return on the bond cash flow, including the bond principal when maturity arrives plus the interest received, and the purchase price. Finally, a bond's yield to call is the bond's cash flow internal rate of return if it is called in by the company at their earliest opportunity.

Bonds yields are unusual in that they vary inversely to the price of the bond. Should a bond price decline, then the yield will rise. If instead the rates of interest drop, then the bond's price will go up in general.

Some securities come with real yields. TIPS are a primary example of this. A real yield means that the face value of the instrument will be adjusted upwards compared to the CPI inflation index. It would then be set against this principal that is adjusted to make certain that an investor makes a better return than the rate of inflation.

This ensures that his or her purchasing power is protected. TIPS are one rare investment that will not allow investors to lose money if they purchased them in the auction and keep them until they mature, either as a result of deflation, meaning falling prices, or inflation, signifying rising prices over time.

Yield to Maturity (YTM)

Yield to Maturity is also widely known in investment and analyst circles by its acronym YTM, as well as by the phrases book yield and redemption yield. This represents the aggregate return which investors can expect to receive for a bond if they keep the security until the end of its actual life. This is why YTM is generally called a longer term bond yield even though it is still expressed as a rate per year. Another way of saying this is that this proves to be the investment's internal rate of return for the bond if the owner keeps it all the way through maturity. This assumes of course that the bond issuer makes all of its payments both on time and in the full amounts contracted.

In order to understand the Yield to Maturity calculations, it is critical to realize that the formula assumes all coupon payments the issuer makes will be exactly reinvested for the rate of the current yield of the bond. The formula similarly considers the bond's par value, current price on the market, term to maturity, and coupon interest rate. All of this makes the YTM a complicated yet good formula for determining the return of a bond. It allows investors to effectively compare and contrast those bonds which possess varying coupon rates and maturity dates.

There are several different ways to figure out the Yield to Maturity. It is a complicated formula so many investors simply fall back on pre-printed and -figured bond yield tables. Determining the exact YTM requires either a software program or the use of a financial or business calculator. This is because the value for a basis point drops as the price for a bond increases in an inverse manner. Many firms actually calculate YTM for six month time frames as well as on an annual basis. They do this because most coupon payments take place twice per year.

A significant difference between Yield to Maturity and the current yield lies in the fact that the YTM takes into account money's time value, while the simplified current yield computations will not. This is why investors often prefer to utilize the YTM instead of the current yield when they are crunching number on bond returns to compare and contrast with other bond issues and different types of investments.

There are a number of similar yet still variations on the classical Yield to

Maturity figure. These should never be confused with the true YTM. Among these are the Yield to call (YTC), Yield to put (YTP), and the Yield to worst (YTW). Yields to call go with the assumption that the bond issuer will recall the bond by repurchasing it in advance of it reaching maturity. This assumes that the resulting cash flow period will be shortened. Yield to put is much like the YTC, only the seller is allowed to and may sell the bond back to its issuer on a specific date for a pre-determined price. Finally, Yield to worst means that the bonds in question can be put, called, or even exchanged. This is why YTW bonds usually have the smallest yields from the three variations on YTM and the YTM rate itself.

There are some important limitations to the utility of Yield to Maturity as a measurement for comparing and contrasting various bonds against other bonds and other forms of investment classes as well. With YTM, these calculations never take into account the actual taxes which investors will have to pay on the bonds. This is why YTM is sometimes called the gross redemption yield. These calculations for yield also do not factor in either selling or buying costs for the bonds themselves.

It is also important to keep in mind that YTM is limited by the fact that both it and current yields are estimate calculations. They can not ever be 100 percent accurate or reliable. The true returns will vary with the realized price of a bond when a holder sells it. The prices of such bonds can vary significantly as the market actually determines them (and not the issuer). Such variations in the value of a bond and the price for which it is sold may impact the YTM substantially. They more drastically impact the current yield calculations and measurement in the end.

Zero Balance Account (ZBA)

The zero balance account, also known by its acronym ZBA, refers to the type of checking account which maintains a permanent balance of zero. The account does this through an automatic transfer of funds out of a master account. The amount which transfers over only proves to be sufficient enough to cover any and all checks which other financial institutions present to the bank where the holder's account resides.

Corporations utilize these zero balance accounts in order to draw down excessive balances from separate accounts. It also helps them to keep better and stricter control over amounts they disburse in the ordinary everyday course of business operations.

These accounts will therefore only have a zero balance within them. The only exception to this zero balance account status is when checks are written against them and presented to the bank in question. In this way, companies are able to keep the balances as close to zero for accounts that do not have any reason to hold excessive reserves. The activity in these ZBA's is restricted to only processing payments. This is why they do not maintain any ongoing balances.

Because of this, a larger sum of funds will remain available for the company to deploy. They can instead put them to work in investments and company cash flow purposes rather than keeping low dollar amounts lying idly by in a number of sub-accounts. It does not present a problem when checks must be paid off from these special zero balance accounts, since the electronic clearing system recognizes that these accounts are in fact ZBA's and they will move the necessary funds over from the master account at the financial institution in the precise dollar amount needed to clear the check.

Companies and other organizations can also rely on a zero balance account to fund purchases which employees make with their debit cards. This allows them to carefully monitor all of the financial transactions and any activities which take place on the cards, since the debits must be pre-authorized. This works well for companies and charitable not for profit organizations which are protected by not maintaining any idle funds within the ZBA's.

The debit card transaction will not be approved by the bank which backs them until and unless the requisite funds become available to the account by a transfer from the authorized account representative at the firm or NGO. This means that debit card transactions simply can not be run without prior authorization by the appropriate superior in the organization. Businesses are able to reduce their risks of activities which are not approved of occurring.

This is critically important to especially larger organizations with many employees and numerous sub accounts and associated corporate debit cards. There is no better spending control oversight for these types of situations than the zero balance account. Incidental charges can be monitored throughout the sizeable operations.

Since incidental expenditures are variable in nature, it is harder to fund and control them without such an account. Large companies and not for profits effectively reduce rapid access to the company or charitable funds with these debit cards. In this way, they have put into place the best practices for approval procedures. It ensures that such procedures will be adhered to in advance of a purchase being made by an employee.

As budget monitoring tools, these ZBA's are also ideal. They may be established as one account per department or business operation. This allows the accountants at the company an easy and fast means of monitoring annual, monthly, and even weekly to daily purchases. The company book keepers are also able to effectively track particular shorter term projects and their financial expenditures by utilizing such a ZBA. Projects which are in jeopardy of running significantly and rapidly over budget also benefit from such accounts. The overseers can maintain control of all purchases by requiring proper approval and notification before the charges take place.

The master account of such zero balance accounts is the critical component of this entire concept. As the central operational center for all fund management in the organization, the account will be employed to disperse funds to all ZBA subaccounts as needed. These master accounts typically include other benefits like better interest rates for balances which they hold.